City
Scriptures

For Zev & Lisa —
citizens of all these places —
hoping it may bemuse —
in friendship —

Murray

City
Scriptures
Modern Jewish Writing

Murray Baumgarten

Harvard University Press
Cambridge, Massachusetts
and London, England
1982

Publication of this book has been aided by a grant from
the Andrew W. Mellon Foundation

Library of Congress Cataloging in Publication Data

Baumgarten, Murray.
    City scriptures.

    Includes bibliographical references and index.
    1.   American literature – Jewish authors – History and criticism.
    2.   Jewish literature – History and criticism.   3.   Jews in literature.
    4.   City and town in literature.   5.   Yiddish language – Influence
    on foreign languages.
I. Title.
PS153.J4B38   809'.8924   81-6879
ISBN 0-674-13278-5   AACR2

For Sheila Korr Baumgarten

Acknowledgments

I would like to take this opportunity to thank the many friends and colleagues who shared their views and responses with me as I wrote this book. I am indebted to my teacher, Abraham S. Halkin, for introducing me to the complexity of Jewish history and as well to conversations with Daniel Aaron, Edward Alexander, Kevin Avruch, Mishael M. Caspi, John O. Jordan, Richard M. Litvak, John H. Miles, Jr., Clive Sinclair, Joseph H. Silverman, and Ruth Wisse for helping me to comprehend some of its dimensions. Joyce Backman's wit often eased the point of her alert and expert stylistic advice. Charles Fineman and Joan Hodgson provided unusually skilled bibliographical assistance. For support in the form of a fellowship, sabbatical time, travel funds, and research assistance, my thanks to the National Endowment for the Humanities, the Humanities Division of the University of California, Santa Cruz, and the Committee on Research of the Academic Senate. I am also indebted to the many students in Jerusalem and California who joined me in analyzing aspects of Jewish thought, literature, and experience.

Several publishers have kindly granted me permission to quote previously published material. My thanks to Carcanet New Press Ltd. for the lines from Dan Pagis' "Written in Pencil in the Sealed Railway Car," in *Selected Poems of T. Carmi and Dan Pagis*, translated by Stephen Mitchell (London, 1976); to Doubleday & Co., for a passage from *The Bintel Brief*, edited by Isaac Metzker (New York, 1971); to New Directions for lines from Rainer Maria Rilke's "Abisag," in *Selected Poems*, translated by J. B. Leishman (New York, 1964); and to Ruth Whitman for permission to use her translation of Isaac Manger's "Abishag Writes A Letter Home," in *An Anthology of Modern Yiddish Poetry*, selected and translated by Ruth Whitman, published by October House (New York, 1966), and reissued by the Education Department, Workmen's Circle, with an introduction by Isaac Bashevis Singer (New York, 1981).

   This book owes its beginnings to conversations about modern Jewish writing with my wife and daughters. I am grateful for their encouragement as well as the pleasure of their participation in my inquiry.

                                                              M. B.

Santa Cruz, California
October 1981

Contents

City
Scriptures

1
An Urban Phenomenon

The diverse materials of the classic texts of modern Jewish writing cluster around an informing myth: the marginal person emerges from the shtetl and seeks a place in the freer, more complex, and cosmopolitan life of the city. Rooted in the urban experience of the modern Jewish writer, this myth articulates the strategies by which the fictional protagonist (and writer) might escape from the traditional tribal realm, as it simultaneously explores the possibilities of citizenship in the newly found civic arena. Paralleling the historical process, the literary work gives it a conscious shape and purpose, defining an ideal city, at the very least a city of imagination, in which protagonist and people might participate in the general enterprise of western culture. This act reflects the modern Jewish status and situation, for if the emancipated Jew is "the first cosmopolite and citizen of the world," he is such by virtue of being both stranger and city man.[1]

City life offers a setting for the exploration of the historical ambiguities of Jewish experience. In the process of emancipation, the city is also the bridge from tradition to modernity. It makes the move from communal status to ethnic and personal identity possible. Acknowledging the possibilities of modern urban life, the freethinker validates the new at the expense of the old; the "conscious pariah"—committed to the difficult process of critical thinking—by contrast attempts to invent ways to bring the values of tradition into the modern world, as part of the effort to devise a coherent history for person and people.

Together, freethinker and pariah constitute the parameters of dialectic choice in these texts and this history. The work of the imagination maps the ways in which Jews have sought to leave the secret, proto-urban culture they invented in exile—and used as part of their traditional resistance to a society eager to convert and in the case of the Nazis exterminate them—to find the supposed freedom of metropolitan life in the modern world. The result is a literature which tests the very qualities that make their quest possible.

If the city is freedom, dignity, activity, and possibility, it is also limiting, and personal experience will surely add potentially imprisoning and degrading to the list of its characteristics. The myth we are considering includes both sets of possibilities. Let us look more closely at the means by which the young man —the protagonist can also be a woman, of course—central to this story discovers that he can escape from his native borough, which I will designate metaphorically as the shtetl of Brooklyn or Brownsville, and make it to the dazzling city of possibility across the water, the island kingdom of Manhattan. We want to see how the modern writer and literary protagonist can cross the bridge from bondage into freedom. How will they pay the cost? We, unlike hero and heroine, know that in all myths tickets to the promised land have to be paid for. And then, our interest piqued by this tale that Northrop Frye would designate a romance, we want to find out if they can be happy in their new environment. Phrasing it in the traditional speech of European Jewry, we want to know the simple answer to a complicated question: If you moved uptown and became a New York Jew, would the Manhattan you were living in still be *golus*, still exile?

These are the dimensions of the world that Alfred Kazin presents in his recent autobiography. When he names it *New York Jew*, he designates his identity as coterminous with the fabled city on the Hudson. He is no longer a Brownsville Jew, born of Russian-Jewish, socialist, immigrant parents; he is not a greenhorn. He names himself a citizen of the greatest city in the United States, whose urban realm is the domain of his self. Kazin is of particular interest in terms of our myth since he is so fully aware of its value and power as a contextualizing model.

As we shall see, he is careful to use it as a point of reference that enables him to effect a comparison between his own life and that of other Americans. The result highlights the ways in which as a Jew he recapitulates many of the experiences of American ethnic groups, while at the same time suggesting the extent to which his is a unique situation. Finally, in dealing with some of the issues and problems raised by the classic American writers of the nineteenth and twentieth centuries, he implies that American Jewish writing takes its place in the democratic tradition they defined and articulated.

The urban myth provides Kazin with the understated irony, the comedy if you will, of the opening sentences of his book. "One dreamlike week in 1942 I published my first book, *On Native Grounds*, became an editor of *The New Republic*, and with my wife, Natasha, moved into a little apartment on Twenty-fourth Street and Lexington. Its casement windows looked out on a shop that sold everything you could possibly need for your horse. From across the street the shop seemed to gleam with silver rein buckles, brightly polished saddles and bridles. In front of the shop stood a prancing, thoroughly affable wooden horse painted bright yellow."[2] Across the street from his apartment, the horseman's shop beams the message of possibility into Kazin's window. Is it a symbol of coming success or American nostalgia projected into the future, like Gatsby's green light? Does it assure Kazin that one bright day he will emerge from the dim light of the subway onto a farm in Dutchess County with land, horses, real property, and all the other appurtenances of the American dream? Or will a modest house in New Rochelle or Scarsdale have to suffice? Perhaps the affable wooden horse will be the Pegasus that brings the poet inspiration, fame, and worldly goods. Then too it may turn out to be nothing more than a Manhattan mockery of Don Quixote's steed, as the unsuspecting reader is forced to play a reluctant Sancho Panza to his dreams of visionary glory. Only time will enable this young American hero to sort out his future, as he approaches his adventure with his young Eve, as only the time of our reading of this remarkable autobiography will make it possible to decide on the exact meanings of this wooden horse prancing outside the window of our expectation.

In the third paragraph, we learn that Kazin began writing his book in "our single room in Brooklyn Heights soon after our wedding at City Hall." It is 1938, and the world is all before him. Even in the retrospective mood of the past tense he uses, Kazin expresses and participates in the elation of that heady moment.

> I had never lived in Manhattan before. In those first few weeks of my "arrival" in the big city I went between my home, my publishers at Lexington and Twenty-eighth and *The New Republic* at Forty-ninth and Madison in a dizzy exaltation mixed with the direst suspicion of what might happen next. Riding away from the office at the "violet hour" in the sudden opulence of wartime, when the incomparable autumn light of New York still hung over the buildings that would soon be shadowed by the faint wartime brownout, I could feel, when the taxi skidded around the circular passageway under the ramp of Grand Central into Fourth Avenue, sensations of personal deliverance that came and went like the light between the arches.

This lyrical passage is a remarkable mixture of exaltation and suspicion. In the opposition between hope and dread, we recognize that strange Jewish characteristic of the writing: delighting in the pleasures of the moment, Kazin does not fully grant its reality. He has grounds for his skepticism. "Riding home at the rush hour, I could taste all the wild distraction of New York in wartime like a first martini. But I missed my long solitary days in the Forty-second Street Library, I was expecting at every moment to be called into the Army, and I was not prepared for so much good fortune."[3] Perhaps Kazin knows that in their long history Jews and good fortune have not often kept company, as perhaps he knows by the retrospective quality of his glance that the coming war will bring the Holocaust. It is his ability to remember, we note, that is at the root of his skepticism and his suspicion.

Exploring what it means to be a citizen of New York, Kazin mints the city as the coin of his good fortune, while recalling that other Jews in other cities have also enjoyed it for a time. He knows that New York's "violet hour"—his second early quotation from Scott Fitzgerald's *Gatsby*—must give way to other times. If Kazin delights in the savor of this moment of urban possibility, he also knows that freedom may bring terror and emancipation may trail anguish after it. It is already there in the epigraph to the book, also from Fitzgerald's great novel: "Anything can happen now that we've slid over this bridge, I thought, anything at all."

Crossing over the bridge from Brownsville with his family to the lower east side of Manhattan, Henry Roth's David Schearl enters upon his experience of possibility, as *Call It Sleep* maps a pattern similar to Kazin's. It is worth noting in passing that the actuality of bridges in the urban geography of New York takes on in these works an eidetic function—as image, symbol, and historical referent. These works remind us of the metaphorical force of bridges, in literature as in life. For the protagonist of our myth, their very existence is a promise of hope that becomes in his imagination a strategy of liberation. Thus, with his Aunt Bertha, David visits the Metropolitan Museum in Manhattan, and in the company of his friends, especially Leo, he begins to explore not only his neighborhood but the margins of the city, encountering some of the forces that shape it.

The quality of his experience is different now, for he is no longer the David who was so desperately lost in Brownsville, fleeing from the acknowledgment of his mother's brief affair with Luter and ending up unable to make himself understood even in the police station. Then he was his mother's son, living out her earlier remark about herself: " 'Here I am. I know there is a church on a certain street to my left, the vegetable market is to my right, behind me are the railroad tracks and the broken rocks, and before me, a few blocks away is a certain store window that has a kind of white-wash on it—and faces in the whitewash, the kind children draw. Within this pale is my America, and if I ventured further I should be lost. In fact,' she laughed, 'were they even to wash that window, I might never find my way home again.' "[4] No longer limited by his mother's experience of the city in terms of her village past, aware now that his home is not the boundary of his identity, David has embarked upon the development and articulation of his person in psychic and geographic terms. As he begins to project a possible identity in terms of his father's role as worker and citydweller, David moves from psychological processes through geographic space into the religious encounter that will determine the possibilities of his life.

For David, Manhattan is freedom and independence, as he roams the streets and discovers the "great light shining in the crack." The sexual frustration of his experiences with Annie in the cellar of the Brownsville apartment house is transformed into the mystical experience with the underground electricity of the trolley. It is on the lower east side that his father also decides he must give his "prayer" some Jewish education. (Similarly, Kazin's father calls his son "my kaddish" in the Yiddish intonation of the Hebrew term that invokes the traditional world of communal remembrance and memorialization after death.) David's initiation into the mystery of the prophetic tongue, and the discovery that the elemental experience of the prophets is still available in the New York of the lower east side, brings him to the crisis and denouement of the novel. It is almost as if Roth were responding to our question about exile by asking if real freedom and emancipation will be felt in sexual and spiritual terms. Or will David always be bound, as his mother and father are, to the imprisonment of the borough and the terrible history they suffer from?

There is other evidence that David Schearl is the New York Jew of this novel. Take the scene after he has thrust the milk dipper onto the third rail and faints from the shock. It is much too long a passage, extraordinary as it is, to quote. But few can forget the remarkable babble of the city's multitudes around him. All the city's people seem to have made an appearance in order to contribute their ethnic phrases to the urban confusion.

Voiced in their native tongues, their shock at David's wound emerges as a graphic demonstration of what Louis Wirth has called "urbanism as a way of life,"[5] which is rendered on the page in a vivid orthographic mode by Roth. These people become an eclectic urban congregation before David Schearl's offering of himself in atonement for his parents' guilt: they respond antiphonally and chorally to the drama of life and death played out before them. Entering the scene to help the wounded boy, the young doctor and Irish policeman arrange the ritual, arraying its participants in concentric circles of concern and intensity. The various groups, rendered brilliantly in terms of their dialects, express their deepest beliefs like a litmus of traditional communal life. None, however, dominates the shape of the ritual; all partake of and donate to it. As if he had become the spirit of this teeming city, the reader experiences the multiple meanings that inform it.

As the various groups disperse to resume their own lives, we realize how they accept instability in the world at large as a norm. Linguists would note the same thing about their dialects. Their own children would later accuse them of not being American enough or speaking proper English, leading to a simplification of the transitional richness of the experience of the older generation in favor of the modernist conformity of younger freethinkers. It is part of Roth's achievement that he articulates an essential quality of urban life in the course of his rendering of the mythic journey of his young protagonist. Comparable to Joyce's, Roth's work is a central example of the city scriptures of the Jews.

What does it mean to be a New York Jew for David? He has taken upon himself, as the mark of his freedom, the effort to comprehend and transform the imprisoning history of his psyche and his parents and, by a heroic act, attempt to heal their familial wounds. He does not simply light out for the wilderness; rather, he confronts the pain and suffering of Brownsville in order to discover new possibilities in Manhattan. The ritual he unconsciously devises has its roots in Isaiah, for the autobiographical moment of recounting of the prophet's vocational marking inspires David's act. As part of his fitful education in Jewish tradition and the holy tongue in cheder, David has studied this passage. It imprints itself upon his imagination, thus becoming an example for his own life. Roth knows of course that this prophetic moment also served to kindle the passion of Jesus that led to Christianity. David's act also echoes his passion. It is important to remember that the congregants in the street include the range of immigrant groups in this enactment of the bubbling pot of the city's multitudinous traditions. The result is not simply an un-Jewish event or a reenactment of the founding moment of the Christian drama. The event is over-determined: the psychological concerns join with urban realities, as the dynamic process of this passage provides us with a model of the possibilities and values of city experience, momentary as it is, that fuse into a brilliant unifying image of personal, sociological, and cultural identity.

David seeks to confront his past and raise it to a new level of consciousness. By contrast with Isaac Bashevis Singer's protagonist Herman Broder in *Enemies, a Love Story*, who experiences a similarly complex agon in encountering his seemingly resurrected first wife on the lower east side, while thinking of the new wife with whom he lives in Coney Island and meeting his mistress in the Bronx, David does not seek to compartmentalize his experiences. Herman abandons all his women and thus himself; David is in search of the act that will yield a coherent identity and continuous history. What has made such liberation possible for David, and by implication for Kazin but not for Herman Broder? Is it that both are young and Herman is older, European? Or that he functions in the city but is never its citizen?

When David puts the dipper into the crack in the street leading to the third rail, he makes contact with the ultimate power of his world and his city. He contacts the electricity that powers the trolleys, the transportation system that makes it one city and gives it shape as an urban landscape. Kazin also understands the function of these images when he describes Grand Central Station at the beginning of his book. For both, the city is transition, an emblem of the possibility of change, be it geographic, personal, social, cultural, or psychic. For David the electric current is one with the angel of the God of Isaiah, who brought the prophet the burning coal that seared his lips at the same moment it brought him the gift and doom of his prophetic vocation. Semioticists might note that the electricity David encounters is the fundamental binary opposition of the code of this city. It is its power for good as well as for evil, the energy that defines it as a city, just as Isaiah's God is the condition and force that makes him human. Herman Broder, by contrast, constantly flirts with absolute power, grappling with ultimate force in quest of self-knowledge, and yet finally refuses to confront it. David's intensity makes him a citizen of his chosen city.[6] Accepting the complexity of his identity, Herman, unlike David, makes a fetish of his own mysteriousness and so escapes from the city in order to maintain his status and person as a wanderer and eternal survivor.

We wonder if that can be the full story, and David's seriousness his secret weapon in the confrontation with the all-inclusive power of Manhattan. Is all it takes a spiritual equivalent of the fancy footwork John Travolta had to learn before he makes good in the film *Saturday Night Fever?* Note the role of the Verazzano Bridge for Travolta's odyssey, in stressing the differences between subsidiary boroughs and the central arena of New York City, thus paralleling for the contemporary world of popular culture possibilities available to David Schearl and Alfred Kazin.

I believe the ultimate secret of the process by which David and Kazin become citizens of this awesome city is linguistic. (Pursuing the semiotic method, we could develop the comparison with Travolta by noting the ways in which dancing is a code like the speech used by the characters of *Call It Sleep*.) If Kazin writes his book as an answer to Henry Adams, another meditator on the century of power, it is important to realize that, in the confrontation with New York as the city of power in the country of power, David and Kazin start not as victims but as equals because they are possessed of the powerful language of the Jews. It is Yiddish—abundant, expressive, subtle—that shields them from the city's brute force. As language and as culture it focuses their world and enables them to make meaning of it.

In Roth's novel, Yiddish is rendered in the graceful and simple English of the family dialogues; English is fractured in the street where it functions as a lingua franca. Roth also knows the ways in which Yiddish is open to Hebrew and allows David to comprehend the prophetic tongue through the native language of European Jewry. Yiddish is there for Kazin in the subtle intonation of his English, and Hebrew is there as well in the exhibit of illuminated manuscripts in Widener Library, where he meets his alienated son at one of the climactic moments of the book. Also, as Kazin watches his father deteriorate into senility, he discovers that he has fixed on one vibrant Hebrew phrase, taken from the morning liturgy that every Jewish boy used to learn by heart, which he repeats over and over. "Lefonecho . . . Before Thy Face I render thanks to Thee, Everlasting King, who has mercifully restored my soul within me; thy faithfulness is great."[7]

The material we are dealing with, like the form it takes, is characterized by its interlinguistic qualities. If these works are written in English, it is a language with Yiddish lurking behind every Anglo-Saxon character. In *A Walker in the City* Kazin maps his experience in bilingual terms, as the lyrical opening sentences carry us from the English of his present into the eternal present of Yiddish. As they flow into each other, the man returns to the childhood that fathered him, and his mother tongue, the *mameloshen*, comes back as the language of his experience. The "old women in their shapeless flowered housedresses and ritual wigs . . . give Brownsville back to me. In their soft dumpy bodies and the unbulging way they occupy the tenement stoops, their hands blankly folded in each other as if they had been sitting on these stoops from the beginning of time, I sense again the old foreboding that all my life would be like this. *Urime Yidn.* Alfred, what do you want of us poor Jews?"[8] Their Yiddish encounters the modernity of English, and the interlinguistic effect defines the consciousness of the narrator for himself and for us. If Yiddish is the mother tongue of the Jews, Hebrew has always been their holy, prophetic, and patriarchal language. The English of these books is their field of play. Thus it defines the Jewish experience of its characters and writers as it allows the ancient language in all its creative force to encounter the power of modernity, refracted by the subtle intonation of the modern language of the European Jews: by Yiddish, no longer jargon or dialect but medium and linguistic magic all its own.

As the city cut the languages and imported cultural baggage of its in-migrating inhabitants along the fault lines of their originating communities, it also offered writer and Jew the opportunity to appropriate the new urban speech patterns and cultural habits that gathered dialect and varied usage into interlinguistic and pluricultural combinations. American Jewish writers thereby marked Brownsville, Brooklyn, "uptown," and later the Bronx, New Rochelle, Scarsdale, Newark, Chicago, and Montreal as their ground. European Jewish writers similarly minted Vienna, Berlin, Prague, Warsaw, Czernowitz, Budapest, and Odessa as the literary arenas of their urban vision, just as their Zionist colleagues defined Tel Aviv and Jerusalem as their cultural focus. To investigate the phenomenon of modern Jewish writing, then, is to participate in the mapping of these boroughs of the imagination and to register the varying choices of the Jewish writer confronting the modern world.

Like the complexities of family life for these new urban inhabitants, the linguistic possibilities are dense and difficult. Few indeed were the speakers of Yiddish who did not also have at least a passing acquaintance with Hebrew, the *l'shon hakodesh*. Folk speech and the sacred Hebrew language of Jewish high culture constantly interpenetrated each other. One of the choices the Jewish writer had to face was the Zionist possibility of writing in Hebrew, the patriarchal tongue, with all that entailed. The range of possibilities and the meaning of linguistic choice become apparent when we realize that S. Y. Agnon, who shared the Nobel Prize for literature in 1966, first wrote in Yiddish before becoming the master of modern Hebrew prose fiction; I. B. Singer, the Yiddish writer who won the Nobel Prize in 1978, began his career as a Hebrew writer; and Saul Bellow, who received the Nobel award in 1976, grew up as a Yiddish speaker and is a masterful translator of its literature, numbering among his accomplishments the brilliant translation of "Gimpel the Fool," the story that first brought Singer's work to the attention of the English reader in 1953. An awareness of the place of Yiddish in the work and life of modern Jewish writers should help to clarify their role in the history of western modernization, as well as to reveal some of the rhetorical sources and linguistic riches of their narrative fiction.

As part of the effort to define a Jewish humanism, these works reconstitute tradition as a usable past in and for the modern present by portraying an ideal city of imagined cultural pluralism. Moving through the interlinguistic combination of its phrases, cultures, and meanings, we experience the vital energy of this volatile mixture. The urban phenomenon that is the result of the tension between the drive for individuality and

the poised forces of the masses, routine, and technology that
assail and threaten the self's very existence; the event that results from poising traditional community of origin against
achieved place in society; the qualitative value that comes into
being when closely related contiguous languages like Yiddish
and Hebrew fuse with English (or German, Russian, Czech,
Hungarian)—*thinking*, in short, in all its pain and difficulty
flares into quickened life. This is not a matter of discipline or
willed effort; it is inherent in the interlinguistic, intercultural
experience of these people. In this world, "only those things are
real whose strength is not impaired but confirmed by thinking.
Neither the freedom of the *schlemiel* and poet nor the innocence
of the suspect nor the escape into nature and art, but thinking is
the new weapon—the only one with which . . . the pariah is endowed . . . in his vital struggle."[9]

What these works do, then, is take us through the process
that establishes the conditions for critical thinking. They do this
by charting the limitations of freethinking in ways that also
echo the enterprise of the classic nineteenth-century American
writers. Writing is the mode in which this version of the problem of thinking takes shape; in reading the modern Jewish writers we discover ourselves once more reclaiming the world of the
Bible, with its anguish and terror of selfhood in the face of a
mindless history. These writers, remake the languages in which
their lives are inscribed by rethinking their meanings. Their
works test modernity in terms of an urban vision of human freedom, taking their places among the efforts of the liberating
imagination in reminding us that tradition is recursive, a dominant presence within and despite the overwhelming power of
the modern. "Even here in this rich country," Louis Simpson
reminds us, "scripture enters."[10]

Focusing on the literary phenomenon with an eye to making
distinctions and discriminations possible, I have tried to ask
what it means that a particular kind of writing has resulted from
the encounter of the Jew and modernity. The effect is to take us
to boundary questions rather than historical exposition or ex-
haustive interpretations of particular writers. In the last ten
years four major works have been published in America, all of
which have a Jewish writer as the central character, who moves

freely between urban center, suburban dispersion, and rural haven. Bellow's *Humboldt's Gift* came out in 1975, Malamud's *Dubin's Lives* in 1979 as did Philip Roth's *The Ghost Writer*; Singer's *Enemies, a Love Story* first appeared in English in 1972, and Johanna Kaplan's *O My America* in 1980. These facts of publishing history suggest that we have reached, if not a conclusion in literary history, then at least a moment of some self-consciousness about the relation between writing, urban life, and the Jew in the modern world that affords us a significant vantage point from which to examine its various aspects.

2
Dual Allegiances

By the middle of the nineteenth century, as Balzac, Dickens, Dostoevsky, Hawthorne, and Melville charted the urban parameters of their respective cultures,[1] there came into being the conditions that would make a modern Jewish literature possible. The status of the Jews changed. Political rights as well as economic and social opportunities were proffered and ratified following Napoleon's 1805 proclamation of emancipation, notably by democratically inclined governments, and literary and cultural imagery was affected. Exotic Rebecca of Scott's *Ivanhoe*, who echoed Shakespeare's Jessica, Shylock's daughter, made way for the kindly Riah of Dickens' *Our Mutual Friend* and George Eliot's Daniel Deronda, with Fagin of *Oliver Twist* serving as the malevolent exception to prove the rule. Jewish emancipation and modernization yielded a linguistic and literary consequence. The Jews became European writers, as Disraeli and Heine defined the intricacies of possible political and artistic careers for their compatriots.

Choosing to participate in the western cultural enterprise, Jews encountered the linguistic possibilities of modernity in having to decide which language to use not only in daily but in professional and even national life. As the holy tongue, Hebrew had pride of place in Jewish culture and had long served as the language of intellectual discourse. Reserved for sacred usage, it nurtured Yiddish, the language of everyday life that most western Jewish writers who grew up in a traditional environment first spoke before they wrote any other European tongue. In the process of linguistic choice, each writer personally recapitulated a people's historical experience.

At one pole, the possibility of freethinking implied the abandonment of the familial language and experience. Learning its codes and employing its languages, the freethinker could buy an entrance ticket to European culture. Alternatively, he might choose to function as a critical thinker and conscious pariah, testing the values, costs, and benefits of freethinking by adopting a skeptical stance and, incorporating the familial language and native meanings into a newly acquired tongue, subtly changing it. His choice marked the possible ranges of political, social, and cultural styles available to him, thereby as well defining the horizon of literary theme, subject, and manner of treatment of his work.

As a fictional character, the freethinker moves through the novels of Bernard Malamud, Saul Bellow, Johanna Kaplan, Henry and Philip Roth, through Bashevis Singer's *The Family Moskat* or his brother's *The Brothers Ashkenazi*, and Sholom Aleichem's "Hodel." It is important to recognize that the boundaries of his effectiveness are limited. Thus, to take one example among many, if Yakov Bok begins by abandoning his prayer shawl and shtetl for the larger world of Kiev where he finds ample food and decent shelter for the first time, by the end of *The Fixer* he has been forced out of his freethinking into a new identification with his people. He rediscovers their values and evaluates his desires in terms of a communal experience, so effectively rendered in Malamud's Yiddish-inflected English. When Bok dreams of killing the tsar, he functions as a radical seeking justice and a place in the world not only for all oppressed groups but in particular for his people. He has ceased being an ideologue and has become a critical thinker. Yakov Bok is not a sophisticated, educated man. For this reason alone, the shift in perception of his identity and role is important, for it highlights the ways in which these are two possibilities available to an entire people as methods of coping with the intertwined processes of emancipation, modernization, and assimilation. By the end of the novel, Bok has become, like Frank Alpine in *The Assistant*, a figure who bridges tradition and the modern world.

Yakov Bok's trajectory is similar to that of many Jewish intellectuals, who begin by defining themselves as freethinkers and then reluctantly conclude that they are still in some way Jews.[2] A moving example of such an encounter between tradition and modernity, showing the unstable freethinker divided against himself, emerges from the pages of Abraham Cahan's Yiddish socialist newspaper, *The Daily Forward*, in 1909.

Dear Mr. Editor:

I was born in a small town in Russia, and until I was sixteen I studied in *Talmud Torahs* and *yeshivas*, but when I came to America I changed quickly. I was influenced by the progressive newspapers, the literature, I developed spiritually and became a freethinker. I meet with freethinking, progressive people, I feel comfortable in their company and agree with their convictions.

But the nature of my feelings is remarkable. Listen to me: Every year when the month of *Elul* rolls around, when the time of *Rosh Hashanah* and *Yom Kippur* approaches, my heart grows heavy and sad. A melancholy descends on me, a longing gnaws at my breast. At that time I cannot rest, I wander about through the streets, lost in thought, depressed.

When I go past a synagogue during these days and hear a cantor chanting the melodies of the prayers, I become very gloomy and my depression is so great that I cannot endure it. My memory goes back to my happy childhood years. I see clearly before me the small town, the fields, the little pond and the woods around it. I recall my childhood friends and our sweet childlike faith. My heart is constricted, and I begin to run like a madman till the tears stream from my eyes and then I become calmer.

These emotions and these moods have become stronger over the years and I decided to go to the synagogue. I went not in order to pray to God but to heal and refresh my aching soul with the cantor's sweet melodies, and this had an unusually good effect on me.

Sitting in the synagogue among *landsleit* and listening to the good cantor, I forgot my unhappy weekday life, the dirty shop, my boss, the bloodsucker, and my pale, sick wife and my children. All of my America with its hurry-up life was forgotten.

I am a member of a Progressive Society, and since I am known there as an outspoken freethinker, they began to criticize me for going to the synagogue. The members do not want to hear of my personal emotions and they won't understand that there are people whose natures are such that memories of their childhood are sometimes stronger than their convictions.

And where can one hide on *Yom Kippur?* There are many of us, like me. They don't go to work, so it would be good if there could be a meeting hall where they could gather to hear a concert, a lecture, or something else.

What is your opinion of this? Awaiting your answer, I remain,

Your reader,
S. R.

America is the condition for freethinking for this letter writer. In the absence of the sheltering institutions of traditional culture, he "developed spiritually." Joining a Progressive Society, as the badge of his modern status, he became an "outspoken freethinker." Even if his new supporting groups are mirrors of the traditional institutions he has left behind, they cannot satisfy him. His willed commitment reveals the crisis of his modernization, caught in the phrase "my unhappy weekday life." His words struggle to comprehend his traditional past in modern America and raise the question of whether traditional and modern values are reconcilable. Intertwined, like reason and emotion, each for him is an unstable solution, which is acknowledged as such by the editor's response.

No one can tell another what to do with himself on *Yom Kippur.* If one is drawn to the synagogue, that is his choice. Naturally, a genuinely sincere freethinker is not drawn to the synagogue. The writer of this letter is full of memories of his childhood days at home, and therefore the cantor's melodies influence him so strongly. Who among us isn't moved by a religious melody remembered from his youth? This, however, has no bearing on loyalty to one's convictions. On *Yom Kippur*, a freethinker can spend his time in a library or with friends. On this day he should not flaunt himself in the eyes of the religious people. There is no sense in arousing their feelings. Every man has a right to live according to his beliefs. The pious man has as much right to his religion as the freethinker to his atheism. To parade one's acts that insult the religious feeling of the pious, especially on *Yom Kippur*, the day they hold most holy, is simply inhuman.[3]

Genuine and sincere, freethinking letter writer and socialist editor cannot jettison the rich cultural past, and yet neither can be satisfied by simply reviving it. Their exchange highlights the freethinker's dilemma. He is emotionally linked to a world that his reasoning has rejected and that his life has allowed him to leave behind. The question is poignant: What is a freethinker to do on Yom Kippur? What culture of the feelings is possible that would allow him to reconcile America, with its hectic life, and the vanished world of yeshiva and talmud torah? Has the price of admission condemned him to the library? Should he become a reform Jew? And what can the editor offer by way of consolation: ideological firmness, not only assimilation into American life but revolutionary transformation, a utopia in which there will be no Jewish question but there will be Yiddish newspapers? The reader believes he has the right to two worlds; the editor claims he should choose the new and, in a tolerant spirit, leave the old behind. To rephrase it in the terms of Cahan's own novelistic account, David Levinsky can rise but he can never return to the easy Jewish identity of his youth. In the portrayal of Levinsky's experience, we recognize his embrace of American capitalism as a serious human loss. Cahan suggests that true socialism will be a modern version of traditional Jewish culture, which Kazin, describing the Friday evening gatherings of relatives and friends over tea and cake, fruitbowl, and radical conversation in *A Walker in the City*, crystallizes into a new version of the Sabbath.[4] Such fusion of traditional and modern is unavailable to the freethinker; for him, spiritual and physical impoverishment result. He experiences what Arendt calls

worldlessness, for he lacks the belief in the reality of either tradition or modernity that would allow him to assert power and
claim a presence. He is not at home in either cultural situation
and so is caught between conflicting worlds.

In assessing the impact of the historical process of Jewish
emancipation and modernization on modern Jewish writing,
critics have turned to prevailing models of social change. Allen
Guttmann, for example, places American Jewish writers on a
spectrum defined by stages of assimilation. "I see the achievements of Emma Lazarus, Abraham Cahan, Meyer Levin, Lud-
wig Lewisohn, Norman Mailer, Saul Bellow, and Philip Roth as
one result of the process of assimilation and its concomitant
crisis of identity." Noting that Bellow's fiction "is in large measure reflexive [and] about the very experiences of which it is the
result," Guttmann concludes that "Bellow's achievement is the
literary climax of a social process."[5] Hannah Arendt, who
draws on parallel sources in the work of Max Weber, focuses
the problem in more explicitly comparative terms. She finds
that modern Jewish writing comprises a hidden tradition because "for over a hundred years the same basic conditions have
obtained and evoked the same basic reaction." Since there are
few links among the great individuals, such as Heinrich Heine,
Sholom Aleichem, Franz Kafka, and Walter Benjamin, the
scholar must elicit the common ground of their varied enterprise. She locates it in a shared political and cultural stance, that
responds to the social tensions elicited by the ambiguous promises of welcome proffered the pariah people of western culture.
These writers, she points out, "were great enough to weave the
strands of their Jewish genius into the general texture of European life" because they were "bold spirits who tried to make of
the emancipation of the Jews that which it really should have
been—an admission of Jews *as Jews* to the ranks of humanity,
rather than a permit to ape the gentiles or an opportunity to
play the parvenu." Each writer seized the limited possibilities of
a narrow Christian culture and made them into the grounds for
a personal humanism, universal in its scope and appeal.[6]

Like Arendt, Guttmann underlines the ironic and ambivalent
aspects of emancipation and assimilation. For both critics, the
resulting marginality of the Jewish writer, who no longer has a

place in his traditional world or a preordained function in the modern realm, makes available special opportunities but at grim personal cost. To rephrase an old Yiddish proverb, he has to find new kinds of weddings to dance at. Or, in the words of Thorstein Veblen, "It appears to be only when the gifted Jew escapes from the cultural environment created and fed by the particular genius of his own people, only when he falls into the alien lines of gentile inquiry and becomes a naturalised, though hyphenate, citizen in the gentile republic of learning, that he comes into his own as a creative leader in the world's intellectual enterprise." Furthermore, "it is by loss of allegiance, or at the best by force of a divided allegiance to the people of his origin, that he finds himself in the vanguard of modern inquiry."[7] The social meanings of the historical process are brought into even sharper focus by Robert Park's phrasing: "When . . . the walls of the medieval ghetto were torn down and the Jew was permitted to participate in the cultural life of the peoples among whom he lived, there appeared" a person "living and sharing intimately in the cultural life and traditions of two distinct peoples; never quite willing to break . . . with his past and his traditions, and not quite accepted, because of racial prejudice, in the new society in which he now sought to find a place. He was a man on the margin of two cultures and two societies."[8] In calling attention to the ways in which the members of the hidden tradition come to a common realization of their situation as social outcasts, Arendt notes that they reflect the political status of all Jews. Though they are intellectuals and perhaps more thoroughly attuned to the demands of the host culture, these individuals are still deeply linked to their native Jewish people and tradition. "It is therefore not surprising," Arendt goes on, "that out of their personal experience Jewish poets, writers, and artists should have been able to evolve the concept of the pariah as a human type."[9] Given the conditions of their social and cultural experience, these Jewish artists enact the same structural role of conscious pariah.

In placing Jewish American writers in the historical process by locating them on a spectrum of developmental phases of emancipation, modernization, and assimilation, Guttmann tends to suggest that the process is inevitable and irreversible.

The earlier writers are more Jewish and less American; the later ones are well on the way to becoming only American. Thus he claims to be charting the history of a literary tradition that is transitional, like the culture whose experiences it reflects. As the literary analogue to the immigrant experience comes to an end, both will be seen as halfway houses on the road to full modernization and Americanization. Guttmann tends to neglect the phase which might suggest that the social process is in fact recursive. He ignores the possibility that the demands of tradition may reappear in different guises in the modern world. If Arendt is right, then her view may lead us to a possible correction of Guttmann's by allowing us to ask whether the conscious-pariah tradition continues. Her structural conceptualization makes possible a dialectical view of historical processes.

What then does it mean to say, as Arendt does, that the conscious pariah is opposed to the parvenu? How are they related to the freethinker? Clearly, the latter emerges when closed, religiously centered communities collide with rationalist thought. The freethinker attempts to escape from his native culture by embracing the new possibilities. The parvenu seeks power in his new cultural amalgam by repudiating his traditional folkways; unlike the freethinker, he does not seek radical transformations but contents himself with political compromises. A critical thinker, the conscious pariah does not attempt to supplant old dispensations with new ones but attempts to salvage potentially humane conditions from existing institutions. Veblen's characterization of the skeptical Jew describes his career: "Intellectually he is likely to become an alien; spiritually he is more than likely to remain a Jew." Veblen emphasizes the fact that there is no easy or apparent way to return home to tradition once the modern enterprise has been broached. "The most amiable share in the gentile community's life that is likely to fall to his lot is that of being interned. One who goes away from home will come to see many unfamiliar things, and to take note of them; but it does not follow that he will swear by all the strange gods whom he meets along the road." His marginality, coupled with his dual allegiance, makes this skeptical Jew a formidable thinker, for "he is in a peculiar degree exposed to the unmediated facts of the current situation; and in a peculiar degree, therefore, he takes his orientation from the run of the facts as he finds them, rather than from the traditional interpretation of analogous facts in the past." The conscious pariah, we can conclude, "is a skeptic by force of circumstances over which he has no control."[10] In attempting to account for them, he is led to do a particular kind of work. He becomes an artist and intellectual because he seeks through his writing to respond to the course of modern Jewish history not only in order to comprehend it as a scholar but in order to come to terms with the experience—the passion, pain, sorrow, and joy—inscribed on body and spirit by the course of these two intertwined histories. He becomes a conscious pariah and critical thinker not by virtue of some historical process that he undergoes and only later reflects upon but instead, as Arendt puts it, he liberates himself by "sheer force of . . . imagination."[11] Therefore, his intellectual accomplishments are central.

One contemporary writer emphasizes the ways in which his marginality led him to artistic vocation. In his "partial autobiography," Richard Stern notes how "I attributed what I thought of as my artist's disposition to the slight displacement from ordinary life which being a Jew allowed me, just as I attributed my distaste for what I thought of as the mundane affairs of my family to my artist's disposition. I liked being a bit of an outsider, not a penalized outsider but a glamorous one."[12] In American fashion his pariah status is the result of social rather than blatant political or economic discrimination. Like Guttmann, who makes explicit the Yiddish sources and Jewish inspiration of much of the best in American Jewish writing, Stern completes the sketch of his own role by noting the importance of this native Jewish language. Bellow, "the first major American novelist who was a Jew, much closer to a traditional Jewish life than mine was," taught him some of "the convolutions of that life and its language—Yiddish. I became conscious of my place not as a Jewish writer but as [one] who was also a Jew even though his material had never been explicitly Jewish."[13] This is the characteristic strategy of the conscious pariah. In choosing to define himself as a maker and actor, he engages the revolutionary role and possibilities of the modern world: self-definition and self-culture through the act of choice. Unlike the freethinker, however, he cannot jettison his past. With Babel, he writes of "things long forgotten."[14]

Before modernization, being Jewish was almost a fact of nature for the Jew. Once he embarked upon the heady voyage of self-discovery, he had to confront the fact that he was now alien to himself; in becoming "other" to himself, he encountered, as did all others involved in the process, the conditions for choice. The Jew now had to enter into the virulent and violent negotiation with his western cohabitants and fellow citizens about the shape and nature of their mutual relationship. When the emancipated Jew chose to speak as both Jew and human being, as citizen of a Yiddish world and member of a European polis, as man or woman, he was asserting his right to participate in a new phase of western and Jewish history and claiming a place for himself and his people in it.

This independence and critical impudence, such literary and historical chutzpah, has made the revolution of modern Jewish writing possible. While retailing the adventures of the Jew in the non-Jewish world, Malamud, Roth, and Bellow, to cite only three American writers in this tradition, have woven together the cloth of a new cultural fabric. It serves as the defense of the imagination[15] against the freethinking advocates of a thoroughgoing modernization and total assimilation, as well as the compromising and often repressive bourgeois culture of the parvenu. Responding to complex social tensions, modern Jewish writing does not make "good Jews" of its readers. Instead, like Roth's Eli the fanatic, it teaches how donning the garb of tradition as a role to be performed in the modern world breeds skepticism, disquiets the neighbors, and creates the conditions for critical thinking.[16]

In speaking out about his ambivalent situation, the critical thinker articulates the situation of the Jew in the modern world and out of worldlessness makes an independent realm. This is the continuo we hear in so much Yiddish poetry, particularly the poems of Manger, in which biblical characters and shtetl types become one and perform this crucial act. A fitting theme for a world ever threatened with destruction, it echoes its bravery in daring even to exist against the odds of history and the Christian majority culture of Europe. Yiddish poets thereby proclaim their right to compete in the international republic of letters with the great European writers. In the sly force of their idiom, the Yiddish writers enact the heroic act of speaking which, as Hannah Arendt points out in *The Human Condition*, implicates them in an encounter with time and history that provides them entry into culture in their own voice and person.[17] In the very texture of their language these writers articulate and confront the general problems of imaginative writing in the modern world, exploring them with a personal, unique, and brilliant intensity. Recognizing the conditions that had brought them to the status of conscious pariahs because they were not allowed entry to Europe as Jews but only as abstract human beings, critical thinkers made them the occasion for the moment of impassioned human speech, and thereby found both western and Jewish purposes for their life and work.

Yiddish, Jewish culture and language, is the enabling condition for and implicit figure in the work of American and European Jewish writers. We can articulate its full meaning only by exploring its effects on their work. Ironically, the hidden tradition is, I believe, determined by a particular linguistic usage and cultural practice. The particular effects, values, and meanings of the work of writers like Heine, Babel, and Henry Roth, for example, are due to the fact that their writings derive from and embody a dual yet intertwined linguistic and cultural allegiance. "The window was open so the skinny bird flew in," Malamud's story "The Jewbird" begins. "Flappity-flap with its frazzled black wings. That's how it goes. It's open, you're in. Closed, you're out and that's your fate." The action of the story elicits the Yiddish undertone of this description, as the Jewbird lands on the dinner table of the Cohen family. "The frozen foods salesman was sitting at supper with his wife and young son on a hot August evening . . . [they] were all in the city after two weeks out because Cohen's mother was dying. They had been enjoying Kingston, New York, but drove back when Mama got sick in her flat in the Bronx." The intertwined English and Yiddish rhythms, which first serve as a statement about the assimilation of the Cohens, separate into the conflicting themes and characters of the story. At its conclusion the Jewbird, who speaks Yiddish, prays "without Book or tallith, but with passion," and serves as the son's tutor and moral instructor, is thrown out of his shelter by the infuriated father (whose dreams have been invaded by the Jewbird) on the same day that the grandmother dies. The Jewbird's death parallels Mama's; the son's tears and his mother's sorrow in the face of the father's brazen, "I threw him out and he flew away. Good riddance," suggest that these punctuating deaths do not mark the end of Yiddish as theme and value for this family but, rather, their preservation in a transformed state, as memory.[18]

In order to articulate the varied range of meanings implicit in this dual allegiance, it is necessary to distinguish between different kinds of marginality. In effect, I am glossing Veblen's distinction between "loss of allegiance" and the "force of a divided allegiance" by pointing to the ways in which the first is the central feature of the freethinker while the second distinguishes the critical thinker, the skeptic of whom Veblen speaks, Arendt's conscious pariah. Examining the conflict in particular narratives between free and critical thinkers, we register their varying responses to the problem of marginality. Implicitly, we also acknowledge their diverse range of audiences and note their ambivalent ontological status.[19]

To accomplish these tasks we need a model for our work of a different order of generalization than the usual historical and sociological one. We need to begin with Park's "cultural hybrid" and then focus on linguistic and cultural issues. Using insights generated by linguists and semioticists, we need, in the words of Michael Halliday, to draw a conceptual framework more from rhetoric than from logic, and to devise "a grammar of choices rather than of rules."[20] Clearly the focus must be comparative and, in its most important sense, literary; at the same time, we should link that to the valuable conceptualizations of recent anthropological inquiries into the ethnography of speaking.[21] In establishing parallels between the social process and linguistic practice, I hope to define the special situation of modern Jewish writers.

It is worth noting, if only in passing, that in the eyes of modern western Jews and non-Jews alike, Yiddish was a pariah culture. The confusion is brought about in part because of its status as an interlinguistic language and culture, formed by Hebrew and the sacred Jewish texts as well as the syntax and vocabulary of medieval German with a varying admixture of Slavic and even English. In seeking to purify the Jews of their Yiddish, Zionists, German Jews, and gentiles intended to rid them of an inherited center and thus welcome them into a thoroughly non-Jewish and more universal realm. In linguistic terms, this became the debate over the status of Yiddish. In that context, the self-conscious assertion of Yiddish writers that the *mameloshen* was not a dialect but a full-fledged language entitling them to a place in the republic of letters amounts to a national, ethnic, religious, and critical claim, directly parallel to that of the conscious pariah.

Unlike the freethinker, the critical thinker does not accept a place on the spectrum of assimilatory stages. Nor, we presume, was our letter writer to *The Daily Forward* satisfied with the editor's advice. There is something about the accent and the Hebrew characters of their writing that makes it impossible for either to slip into the anonymous mass of American society: they need their Progressive Society of freethinking Jews just as Asa Heshel Bannet needs his in *The Family Moskat*.

Like Bashevis Singer though in a different mode, Hannah Arendt tests, evaluates, and in the best sense of the word *proves* the ideological strategies proposed for coping with the Jewish situation in the modern world.

Such an activity is healthy because it is critical; it is experimental in the sense that it takes these strategies as hypotheses, whether they emerge from traditional Judaism or the coffee-houses of Vienna, and subjects them to the felt experience of poetry, fiction, or history. In the process, the writer, fabler, or historian examines the tradition first articulated by Spinoza, who proved by his theorems that God and love are perhaps the same and that they are everywhere. As Bashevis Singer puts it in his modern version of an older story:

> Dr. Fischelson looked up at the sky. The black arch was thickly sown with stars—there were green, red, yellow, blue stars; there were large ones and small ones, winking and steady ones. There were those that were clustered in dense groups and those that were alone. In the higher

sphere, apparently, little notice was taken of the fact that a certain Dr. Fischelson had in his declining days married someone called Black Dobbe. Seen from above even the Great War was nothing but a temporary play of the modes . . . Yes, the divine substance was extended and had neither beginning nor end; it was absolute, indivisible, eternal, without duration, infinite in its attributes. Its waves and bubbles danced in the universal cauldron, seething with change, following the unbroken chain of causes and effects, and he, Dr. Fischelson, with his unavoidable fate, was part of this. The doctor closed his eyelids and allowed the breeze to cool the sweat on his forehead and stir the hair of his beard. He breathed deeply of the midnight air, supported his shaky hands on the window sill and murmured, "Divine Spinoza, forgive me. I have become a fool."[22]

Only a critical thinker can comprehend the comedy of freethinking, for the instability and willed choice of the freethinker is the enabling condition of the former's discoveries. Reading this passage from "The Spinoza of Market Street," we encounter the structural irony of the critical thinker's situation. Inhabiting both the Jewish and the modern world at the same time, he discovers who he is in observing their conflict in his own person at the moment of crisis. As readers, we play both sides of the role, identifying with the letter-writing freethinker and the critical editor, just as we become the Dr. Fischelson who is at once an avatar of Spinoza and a foolish *senex amans*. We too are forced to confront the inescapable ironies of the interaction.

In testing western ideals and ideologies of modernization and assimilation in an empirical way, the modern Jewish writer implicitly values the Jewish habits against which these modernizing strategies are measured. The experience, which these ideologies are to transform, turns out to be richer in meaning and value, than the forceful abstractions aggressively invading it in the name of modernity. In effect, we are charting the trajectories and values of an ironic mode of literature. Its tonalities grow from conditions basic to the crisis of modern and Jewish culture, and its ironic effects derive from the imaginative re-

sponse of the conscious pariah to them. Such a response is not
confined to literature, but, in that special habit of the Jews, the
people of the book, it enters as an active principle into the world
of everyday reality.

Just as the Jew must reconcile the demands of book and life,
so the critical thinker needs to resolve the tensions arising from
his dual allegiance. If the Torah has been a Jewish version of the
Kantian categories of space and time projected from the mind
onto reality and endows it with an intelligible shape and meaning, so does Yiddish transform the modern language in which
the Jewish writer functions. The pressure of Yiddish with, as
Bashevis Singer describes it, its greater supply of vitamins[23]
makes itself felt everywhere in modern Jewish writing. We hear
it in Malamud's "Jewbird," in Portnoy's aggravation, in the
winding nuances of Babel's "Gedali," as well as in Herzog's self-
parodying letters. They can almost be called translations from
the Yiddish. In these novels and stories, as in Heine's poem to
the Sabbath Princess, character, situation, and voice, rooted in
the semiautonomous life of the European Jewish culture that
nurtured its own way of speech, invade the modern European
languages and literatures and render them, through the comic
irony of the weak overcoming the strong, helpless before the
force of the Jewish imagination. To paraphrase Walter Benjamin, Yiddish shines through their syntax.[24] Philip Roth uses
this fact to characterize the American Jewish writer who is one
of the protagonists of his novel, *The Ghost Writer*. Roth says of
E. I. Lonoff, a fictional portrayal in part of Malamud and I. B.
Singer, that he would always be dismissed by the critics "as
some quaint remnant of the Old World ghetto, an out-of-step
folklorist pathetically oblivious of the major currents of literature and society." He is a mysterious recluse. "Even among his
readers there had been some who thought that E. I. Lonoff's
fantasies about Americans had been written in Yiddish some-
where inside Czarist Russia before he supposedly died there (as
in fact his father had nearly perished) from injuries suffered in a
pogrom."[25] To recognize this fact of dual allegiance is to acknowledge the ways in which modern Jewish writing is a chapter in what Max and Uriel Weinreich called the history of Jewish
interlinguistics, just as the interaction of Aramaic and Hebrew
centuries ago informed another vital era of Jewish life.

To multiply examples by listing passages in which Yiddish words and phrases are the pivots of meaning in works written in the modern Western languages is insufficient evidence. Certain Yiddish words have in fact been effectively assimilated into American English, in part as a result of the interlinguistic process. What we need to focus on is the effect of combination, when lexical borrowing is reinforced by character as well as syntax and narrative voicing; the full situation functions to evoke the panoply of the values of Yiddish culture. We encounter it, for example, when the narrator of Isaac Babel's "Gedali," from that astonishing collection he published in 1929, *Red Cavalry*, engages his newly found friend in a conversation about the meanings of the Revolution.

The narrator of the story is lyrically evoking his search for his past. "O the rotted Talmuds of my childhood!" he exclaims, "O the dense melancholy of memories!" In old Gedali, "the little proprietor in smoked glasses" of a curiosity shop, he discovers someone who allows him to respond to his past not as a collection of objects that he can observe, assess, and put away—that is, as a freethinker who can leave behind his past—but as a group of roles, habits, lifestyles, and individuals of which his own identity is composed. It is no surprise that Gedali evokes his Jewish past for the narrator. What is striking is the way in which Gedali makes it possible for the narrator to experience an alternate vision of history: in the shocking conclusion of the story, narrator and reader discover and participate not in the revolutionary order of communism but in the "impossible International" of the Sabbath.

Babel chose to write in Russian, in a startling idiolect of vividly colored objects and events, of sharp hypnotic images blending into each other like an Eisenstein film montage. Saul Bellow wonders what it means for Babel to have made such a choice. Why not Yiddish, Bellow asks, with an intensity that makes us raise the same question about Bellow himself, the brilliant translator of *Gimpel the Fool*. The American writer's characterization of the Russian writer's choice underscores the interlinguistic situation of the Jewish writer in the modern world. As Bellow comments, "Before he disappeared from view during one of Stalin's purges, Babel had been put in charge of publishing the works of Sholom Aleichem in Yiddish. Why should he have chosen therefore to write his own stories in Russian, the language of the oppressors, of Pobedonostev and the Black Hundreds? . . . He wrote in Russian from motives we can never expect to understand fully."[26] Nevertheless, the interlinguistic, intercultural context of this choice is clear.

In "Awakening," Babel tells us how as a young boy considering a literary vocation, he discovered he had no words for the trees and flowers he wanted to write about; only after learning their Russian names from an older friend was he launched upon his career. Like Bellow, Babel is in pursuit of a western ideal and vocation, and his literary ambition is part and parcel of his desire to express his identity as a fully emancipated European. But Yiddish remains as the subtext of the Russian. "Gedali" is drenched in its supple nuances. " 'Gedali,' I said, 'today is Friday, and it's already evening. Where are Jewish biscuits to be got, and a Jewish glass of tea, and a little of that pensioned-off God in a glass of tea?' "[27] The words may be Russian, but the touch of the hands is Yiddish. The narrator, whose role in this story is a result of his willed, modernist, freethinking separation from Yiddish and Jewish culture, is on the way to rediscovering his mother culture. The story dramatizes the process of mythic reidentification in a gesture of profound psychological meaning. Speaking to Gedali in these accents evokes the language the narrator's grandmother used in "Awakening" to protect him from his father's anger when the young boy refused to study the violin and become another Heifetz.[28]

Separation has led not only to critical assessment of his engagement in modern revolutionary activity, but ironically to a rediscovery of the abiding value in the original familial experience. The hasidic outfit in Roth's "Eli the Fanatic," the Yiddish and Hebrew words in the late poems of Heine, the meandering subtleties of Yiddish speech rhythms in Malamud's "Jewbird," all lead to the shock of recognition: the folkways that the modern world shatters still exist not only as personal memories but as transcendent human values. Though we are distant from that traditional culture and cannot embrace it, we cannot dispense with it. Instead, we must account for its presence and continuous pressure, as language and cultural value. This Jewish humanism lurks behind the Russian of Babel's stories in their

echoes of Yiddish, which we hear as well in the writing of Malamud, Bellow, Kaplan, and Roth. The interaction of modern and
traditional values is underscored by their common Yiddish
continuo.

It is important to note that the individual passes out of his or
her original community and yet is measured by the ability to
remember it. Leaving behind old habits, the critical thinker
takes along old values. Self-definition depends on the honoring
of two commitments: his independence can be maintained only
insofar as he recognizes his traditional values. He must continue
the search for a new order within himself that reconciles past
and present and fits both to the modern framework. His dual
allegiance leads the modern Jewish writer to an intensive exploration of the conditions for character and individuality.

3
Clothing and Character

Commenting on the achievement of modern Jewish writers, Richard Stern compares it to the nineteenth-century New England writers. Like Hawthorne and Melville, he points out, Malamud and Bellow share a commitment to ideas. Nevertheless, in both instances it does not yield works of utopian speculation and fantasy: these novels stay "grounded in the real." Stern bases his assessment on an observation about their common interest in character. Unlike Mann, Joyce, and Proust, who relegated it to the margins of their art, "character is back in the middle" of these American and Jewish novels.[1] One way of amplifying and examining this insight is to ask how this recovery of character by Jewish writers may be compared to the practice of the New England novelists. Is the interlinguistic history of the former, and their dual allegiances, a situation shared with the latter? Is it appropriate even to parallel the New England Renaissance with an American Jewish one? In neither instance can we claim the invention of the idea of character in the novel as such but, more interestingly, can point to the fact that in both there occurred a systematic and profound exploration of the conditions for its existence. The question we must therefore address is what cultural process made this possible.

Emerging late from traditional society, modern Jews replayed the modernization process, so that character and individualism, emerging out of the stage of secularism, had not only a positive but a necessary value for them. In this they parallel the enter-

prise of the New England writers. For them, too, the free-
thinker/critical thinker dialectic grew out of the encounter of a
traditional culture and the modernizing circumstances of the
new world. Like the New England writers, the Jewish writers
gain the idea of character from the historical crisis that their traditional culture undergoes, and which produces not only their
access to western literary prowess but the rise of Yiddish and
Hebrew literature as well. As Bellow and Henry Roth, for example, consciously center their work on the crisis of modernization in which they are centrally implicated as Jews, they also
reenact a process of vital significance to the classic New England
writers as well. In terms of the process of modernization, the
two groups play parallel roles: both focus their narratives on
the tension between freethinkers, who, rejecting their traditional religious culture, are yet irresistibly drawn to its structures, and the critical thinker, who cannot simply abandon his
past in the hope of choosing and making a new self. The writers
of the American Renaissance, like the modern Jewish writers,
emerged from a religious culture centered on the notion of elec-
tion, on the idea of their chosenness; and both work with a language of tradition while seeking to articulate an idiolect expressive of a critical view of their communal religious past and their
modern individualist present in response to the crisis of mod-
dernity.

We can detect the force of this crisis in modern Jewish writing
in the ways in which Yiddish remains a covert theme, subject,
and linguistic presence. Consider, for example, the conflict of
languages in Henry Roth's *Call It Sleep,* in which the meeting
ground of the street is an arena where everybody frames his or
her English according to their native tongue. Polish, Yiddish,
Italian, and Irish folk all communicate in the lingua franca of a
common but in each case differently inflected pidgin English.
But at home David Schearl and his family speak an elegant and
expressive Yiddish rich in nuance and feeling. For them, English
as language and vehicle of American culture interferes with
their Yiddish world. The ironies are manifold, however, for
both Albert and Genya have felt profound dissatisfaction with
their native culture; the Yiddish world of the shtetl has not been
able to fill their needs, and even before they leave for America,

both of them violate some of the deepest values of their traditional cultures: Albert almost batters his father to death, and Genya becomes sexually involved with a church organist. The Yiddish arena of their American home continues to be a battleground of mutual suspicion, envy, and unsatisfied demands. It is this world that David flees, reenacting his parents' exit from family and traditional culture. Making friends with non-Jews, David discovers the modern values of secondary relationships. The crisis of the novel occurs when the rosary that Leo has given him as a sign of their friendship falls out of his pocket, just as his father has learned of David's discovery of the possibility that he is not Albert's but the organist's child. Driven from home by the threat of a beating, David seeks to confront the overwhelming power of the electric trolley—a surrogate for his father surely—by putting his father's milk ladle against the third rail, whose force he has identified not with his traditional home or his modern world but with a biblical text he learned in cheder. For him, redemption is recursive, and electric power is a version of the coal the angel brings down from heaven to purify Isaiah.

David's is a Jewish odyssey, as he wanders through the city in search of his identity. He reverses his father's experience: David directs his anger toward himself. The crisis of his world propels him into exploration of his own identity rather than blaming his father for his shortcomings: David must face the terror of his history by confronting the terror of selfhood. Modeling his novel on Joyce's *Ulysses*, Henry Roth was also deeply aware of Freud as he wrote this book, and the novel's epiphany has a biblical resonance. If Isaiah like Moses became a stutterer, David at the end of the novel is injured on the ankle and perhaps will limp like a modern Oedipus. In each instance, the terms of the crisis reinforce the commitment to resolving personal contradictions. They move each protagonist to define himself through a powerful symbolic gesture, so that character and fate may become reunited even in the fragmented modern world.

This is not the only instance of the exploration of character in modern Jewish writing, though it is in some ways representative. If David is a Jewish Ulysses, he is also a Yiddish Stephen

Daedalus. The artist is here in search of himself not as prophet or craftsman but as person; he seeks to discover how he can make of the limited entrance ticket to western culture that he has been given by its ambiguous promises a real liberation. Can he in his own person reconcile the demands of two cultures? Is he to be a freethinker, repudiating one in order to embrace the other, or is another alternative possible? We wonder if he can deal with his past so that it does not become a stone around his neck and yet is not merely something that he tries to drop off along the way in order to run the race of modernization unencumbered by the baggage of history.

One of the ways in which these issues unfold in novels like *Call It Sleep* is through an exploration of the meaning of clothing, where it becomes an index of status, as it was in traditional society, and a badge of identity, as the freethinker believes. His suspicion that merely changing clothes provides not just a disguise but initiates the complete transformation of language, values, and lifestyle is a constant possibility. Given this historical context, Henry Roth characterizes the different groups of immigrants aboard the *Peter Stuyvesant* en route to Manhattan by associating each of them with a bit of typical clothing.

> It was May of the year 1907, the year that was destined to bring the greatest number of immigrants to the shores of the United States. All that day, as on all the days since spring began, her decks had been thronged by hundreds upon hundreds of foreigners, natives from almost every land in the world, the joweled close-cropped Teuton, the full-bearded Russian, the scraggly-whiskered Jew, and among them Slovack peasants with docile faces, smooth-cheeked and swarthy Armenians, pimply Greeks, Danes with wrinkled eyelids. All day her decks had been colorful, a matrix of the vivid costumes of other lands, the speckled green-and-yellow aprons, the flowered kerchief, embroidered homespun, the silver-braided sheepskin vest, the gaudy scarfs, yellow boots, fur caps, caftans, dull gabardines.[2]

Portraying the immigrants in terms of facial hair and clothing in the second paragraph of the novel, Roth establishes these two features thematically: the novel will highlight human changes in terms of social appearance.

The rest of the prologue centers on this metonymic theme. Albert Schearl meets his newly arrived wife and son and travels with them from Ellis Island to the Manhattan docks. His embarrassment at being in their company focuses on the blue hat his son is wearing. Its color echoes the blue-coated customs officials to whom his wife has lied about his son's age, reinforcing Albert's unease as to the actual paternity of his son. Furthermore, the fact that his son is wearing a hat at all marks their Jewishness. Trailing polka-dotted ribbons, it also reveals the mother's displacement of her feminine interest in self-ornamentation to her son. Later in the novel this will be developed into one of the contributing causes of David's timidity.

Shortly after they see the Statue of Liberty, ironically described, Albert scoops the hat from the boy's head and sends it "sailing over the ship's side to the green waters below." He justifies his action with the abrasive remark, "You should have left it behind." The child sobs, the mother's gaze wanders. "In the silvery-green wake that curved trumpet-wise through the water, the blue hat still bobbed and rolled, ribbon stretched out on the waves." It becomes an emblem of the hopes and desires of this small family embarking on "that vast incredible land, the land of freedom, of immense opportunity, that Golden Land"[3] with all their psychic baggage of half-consummated dreams, fears, and fragmented histories. Clothing here becomes an index to psychology and character definition, as well as a way of expressing the family conflicts that power the novel's plot.

The ways in which this theme functions for modern Jewish writers as part of their urban experience is one of the major differences between their work and that of the classic American writers. For the Jewish writer, the modern city is a psychic geography; for the New England writer the opposition is not between home-as-shtetl and the city, but between the village and the wilderness. In both instances, the dialectic between the two poles is the central focus. When the Jewish protagonist arranges his appearance by dressing up, he echoes the Puritan hero seeking to discover whether or not his self and moral values are more than a function of his environment. Hester

Prynne's scarlet letter becomes emblem, symbol, and appearance of the ambiguity of language and clothing, as they encode the problematics of choice. This *A* becomes the mark of Hester's identity and self-definition in all its complexity. Like David Schearl's search for identity, Hester's *A* acquires the electric force of language open to multiple readings.

Similarly when Levinsky shaves off his beard in Cahan's *The Rise of David Levinsky*, abandons his traditional Jewish dress, and dons American clothes, he marks his new identity. He has chosen an American self. The course of the novel reveals the implications of this choice. His decision, it turns out, has resulted from weakness rather than strength of character. Adapting himself to his new environment, Levinsky acquires new habits along with new clothes. Communal ties and habits disappear as easily as his old clothes and beard, and he embarks on his career as a rising capitalist: he will be a person defined by upward social mobility.

Like David meditating on the sources of his success, the reader is led into an almost endless regression in the search for the moment of choice that defined the dimensions of Levinsky's self. Did the moment of changing his clothes shape him? His act in that instance, we come to learn, was preceded by his decision to come to America. That decision, however, turns out to have been occasioned by a prior choice, involving Levinsky with Matilda, his non-Jewish friend, who encourages him to leave Russia and, lending him passage money, all but puts him on the boat. Was the crucial decision, then, to listen to her advice, or, before that, simply to seek out her friendship for its own sake? That too turns out to be inevitable, given the circumstances of his childhood, his mother's passion to make him a learned member of the Jewish community, and her self-sacrifice to a pogrom mob in order to save him. When David is left an orphan, some of his mother's ideals and hopes for him remain for a time, but without her active encouragement it is easy to forget them.

As David muses over his past, he finds only vague memories and a sense of unease, but never particular events or traumatic moments: all his life is seemingly part of the flow of event and circumstance. In effect, David has no self; he is only a reflection of his environment and, like a chameleon, takes on new hues to fit in with the surroundings. Protecting himself, he ends up defending an empty fortress. Nowhere is this clearer than in Levinsky's various unsatisfactory relationships with women. David moves from the hands of his mother, to Matilda, to various other chance encounters, yet never manages to commit himself to marriage and the continuation of his name.[4] It is possible to speculate about the effect of the absent father figure on him (his father died when he was a child) and also to see David as a figure without any values of his own to pass on to future generations.

As a self-proclaimed freethinker, David seeks to define himself by choosing narrowly: he becomes nothing more than his function. He is only his professional self in the stage of primitive capital accumulation. Unable to connect past and present, he disrupts his identity and, as a result, has no future. So he does not marry and has no children, the saddest of all destinies for the immigrant community. Perhaps we have here a novelist's comment on Marx's attempt to envisage the end of history, as put into practice by so many of his fellow freethinking Jews when they fell to the seductions of modernity. Without the intercultural tension between traditional sources and modern functions, David becomes rootless, univalent in meaning, and distinctly—for all his money—a nonelectric being.

The Rise of David Levinsky is a novel about the absence of character. It is a study of the impact of modernization on a young man who comes to America ready to accept a behaviorist's definition of self, society, and culture. Levinsky tells his story in the first person, and in the growing sorrow that accompanies his financial triumph we have the ironic truth of this portrait. Cahan's novel is a commentary on the experience of his generation, an ironic response to the consequence of the demise of traditional society's authority on his fellow Jews and Americans. As a socialist, he charted a third possibility and worked for the founding of a different kind of authority from either the traditional or capitalist ones Levinsky experiences. Between the ancient definition of the Jew as chosen or the more recent Jew as entrepreneur, Cahan proposed that they be comrades. Putting aside the garb of tradition, Levinsky dons the capitalist's suit and tie. In changing his clothing he loses his self, which he might have found, Cahan assumes, in wearing worker's jeans. It is worth noting that with this novel Cahan became one of the first recognized American Jewish writers, welcomed into the literary brotherhood of American letters by no less a figure than William Dean Howells, who in *A Hazard of New Fortunes* explores the grounds of his own incipient socialism.

Writing of the violent Parisian mob during the French Revolution, over and over again Thomas Carlyle returns in his great *Sartor Resartus* to the meaning of changing clothes. He is in awe of the furious energy with which the sans-culottes demand that the world abolish distinctions of dress. Sweeping away hierarchical differences, they demand in the name of democracy that the world wear breeches, "jeans"—something it would take an American Jewish manufacturer to bring about some eighty years later. Carlyle shows us how clothes are symbolic veils through which we apprehend the significance of the choices made in wearing them. His is a theme highly appropriate to the transformations brought by modernization—which began in England with the industrialization of the weaving process and was focused symbolically by the Luddites as well as the sans-culottes on the manufacture and meaning of clothing. It is a fact of history that the Jewish immigrant, coming to England or America in the early years of the twentieth century, was drawn to the garment industry, which his labor helped to found and endow with its modern shape. The manufacture of clothing and the consequences of changing his clothes were central to his encounter with the process of modernization. A few generations later, as his children spread through other strata in American culture and concentrated heavily in the liberal professions, university teaching, journalism, film, radio, and television, Americans like Richard Nixon began to wonder if the Jew had succeeded also in industrializing the production of personal identity. Had that too become an urban, and therefore changeable, commodity?

It is fitting, then, to look at the different ways clothing figures in modern Jewish writing. At best it will be an index to the adaptation of the individual to modernization; at worst it will amuse and serve to while away the hours as a fashion show does—or is part of the function of clothing in modern Jewish novels to emphasize the possibilities available to us, their readers, in trying out new selves with a new suit or skirt? How strange that one of the most striking of recent tales dealing with clothing, Philip Roth's "Eli the Fanatic," charts the reversal of the change of clothing and self detailed in David Levinsky's story. Sixty years after Cahan's novel, Roth's story reverses the process: Eli, the young, sensitive lawyer, removes his commuter's tie and jacket; by the end, he has put on the traditional full-length black suit, tie, and black shoes of the hasid of Eastern Europe. And despite the certainty of his friends that Eli has flipped, his change of clothing signals not confusion of personality but assertion of character and choice. In marching down Woodenton's main street, going to the hospital to see his newborn son, Eli asserts his newfound sense of identity: he has marked himself by these actions. In parading forth his identification with his people and heritage, Eli has become, in the eyes of his assimilating Jewish friends in their sanitized suburb, a fanatic.

A similar transformation happens to Yakov Bok in Malamud's *The Fixer*. In this novel, two changes of clothing produce two possible selves for Bok. The first finds him exchanging his hasidic garb and the shtetl, which in the words of his father-in-law Shmuel has everything the outside world does but also is blessed with the presence of God—not known for his presence and civilizing influence in tsarist Russia at large—for the clothes of a Russian peasant. As if to emphasize the truth of Shmuel's words, Bok's prayer shawl and phylacteries slip from his pack as he crosses the river that takes him from the Pale into the holy city of Kiev, forbidden to Jews.

In the course of his short career as a Russian worker, Yakov Bok is accused of blood libel. During his imprisonment, he is systematically harassed and must constantly resist the demand that he confess to the crime, which of course he has not committed, of killing a Christian child and using its blood for Passover matzos. A different miracle from the ironic one of the Prioress' account in the *Canterbury Tales* occurs to Bok. Rejecting the demand that he accept the medieval definition of himself as a Jew, that is, as Christ-killer, refusing to sign the confession that might set him free but would condemn his people, Bok learns who he truly is. His jailors transform him into the Jew he thought he had left behind when he came to Kiev; he is dressed in the traditional black suit, with a prayer shawl added for the occasion; his new beard and earlocks complete the transformation. Like Eli, Yakov fulfills himself by choosing to accept the meaning of this old/new attire. It becomes the badge of his courage and the emblem of his ability to resist a threatened empire's attempt to make him and his people its scapegoat.

Bok begins urban life as a freethinker, perusing the writings of Spinoza by candlelight during his brief time as an apparent Russian in Kiev, and ends his stay in prison as a committed Jewish nationalist. Near the end of the novel, he dreams of meeting the tsar and, after a heated discussion on the injustice of his imprisonment and the treatment of his people, Yakov imagines that he shoots Nicholas. It is as a wronged Jew that he has his revenge, expressing his people's frustration through direct action in a fictional evocation of historical reality. As his name, which means average man, dummy and scapegoat, implies, Bok is not a Jewish intellectual, and Malamud in his person articulates the experience of the toiling Jewish masses as well as demonstrating the need for a mass Jewish politics.

Bok discovers that he cannot escape from himself merely by changing clothes. Even in the modern world of the big city, he cannot simply blend in. Despite the rigors and miseries of prison life, he refuses to commit suicide; his desired transformation of self, with all that it implies of the possibility of enough food, decent shelter, and the right to find a sexual partner, remains the ideal to which he clings. Yet the personal course he undergoes makes him question the earlier premises that guided his actions. In leaving the shtetl and abandoning Shmuel, he has refused the role of pious Aeneas; in Kiev, he encounters a willing Dido but discovers that his Jewish self is repulsed by the thought of intercourse during her menstrual period. He manages to acquire food and reasonable shelter but eats by himself, with only Spinoza for company. In effect, his hopes are founded on illusory assumptions, whose epitome is the idea that in changing clothes he can truly change himself.

The dialectic of clothing changes in this novel parallels that of another Jacob, in Bashevis Singer's *The Slave*. There too Jacob is stripped of his clothes and becomes a Polish peasant, imprisoned and isolated. In both instances, this seeming transformation is the condition for the two Jacobs to begin the struggle with themselves and their fate that issues in their renaming: they become Israel. This struggle centers on possible sexual encounters with the available non-Jewish woman. In both novels, Jacob struggles to make his passion coherent and meaningful— that is, so that he can continue to have a self and a significant story for his life.

Storytelling, as Bellow tells us, is the crucial recourse for a less than powerful individual. For these characters, being able to make a coherent story out of the fragments and contradictions of their lives is the prerequisite for a meaningful identity. "In defeat, a story contains the hope of vindication, of justice. The storyteller is able to make others accept his version of things. And in the stories of the Jewish tradition the world, and even the universe have a human meaning."[5] This is surely one of the reasons that self-presentation is a central feature of modern Jewish writing.

The situation is consistently ironic; the possibility of a meaningful identity arising out of the conflict of tradition and modernity tends always to be a matter of individual tenacity. The strong person, measured perhaps by the depth of his roots in traditional culture, has the chance to have an identity in the modern world insofar as he is willing to confront the absurdity and comedy of the effort. He cannot like Young Goodman Brown accept the either/or alternative—viewing personality in terms either of tradition or modernity—but needs to comprehend the dialectical relation of the two and accept his shifting roles in it.

It is not a matter of a habit or a particular suit of clothes. The personality here is characterized by the ability to choose various possibilities rather than relinquishing the demands of selfhood for the security of ideological armor. Bok and Jacob are forced to cross many boundaries, spiritual as well as geographic. The act of choosing a fate is thrust upon them by their adventures, as both stubbornly and almost to the bitter end resist the definitions of self thrust upon them in order to honor a more complex vision.

In both instances, Jacob-Israel passes on a political legacy in the discovery of the crucial need for a personal political choosing that parallels a national one. Thus Bok acts to preserve his personal integrity and therefore also makes a political choice for his people; Jacob, fighting and running from Pilitzky's men in *The Slave*, is saving himself, his son, and their future by initiating resistance, a fitting prelude to his later religious Zionism. In both novels, Jacob's name and situation prepare him and us for his transformation into the biblical Israel in the modern world, and it is this shift in possibilities that forms the half-visible model for these stories and their characters. The freethinker may act rationally and change his clothes; that serves in these novels as the condition for choice. But the major characters choose to define their individuality not in defiance of the group but in associating themselves with the fate of their community, to which they return like prodigal sons.

These novels focus the question of character and national survival in terms of the desperation of modern Jewish history, punctuated and almost ended by the Holocaust. The clothing theme resonates against the naked bodies of the Jewish dead—stripped, degraded, gassed, poisoned, and shot in an effort to exterminate from the world the very possibility of Jewish identity and selfhood. The nakedness of the Jew before the onslaught of this history functions as a grim reminder of the possibilities of modernity.

"Eli the Fanatic" is set just after World War II, when American Jews, finally allowed into WASP enclaves, escaped to the suburbs at the price of appearing like their Protestant neighbors; they underwent the ordeal of civility while Bok and Jacob were tested through more direct confrontations. These tales are focused on the necessary effort to maintain an awareness of the Holocaust as one possible outcome of modernity. The two Jacobs and Eli resist: their new identity is so strong because it is founded on the recovery of the experience of their historical identity. Thus, when Eli at the end of the story is tranquilized with an injection, Roth concludes: "The drug calmed his soul, but did not touch it down where the blackness had reached."[6]

The protagonists of these works encounter the double bind of their modern situation.

Eli and Bok resolve their personal crisis by defining themselves as conscious pariahs, a stance that has immediate consequences for their lives. In one of the most moving scenes of *The Fixer*, Yakov's wife visits him in prison. She informs him that she has had a son by another man. Married for over six years, she and Yakov had no children, and the explanation for Yakov's sterility, whether due to a lack of protein or the inability to assert himself, here becomes symbolic. Yakov defines his manhood in prison as part of his discovery of himself by formally acknowledging the boy as his own. Similarly, Eli visits his newborn son in the hospital in his hasidic outfit. It is a statement of the boy's heritage. Though his genteel wife cannot comprehend the meaning of his actions, Eli is clear about them. "No, even Eckman [his therapist] wouldn't make him take it off! No! He'd wear it, if he chose to. He'd make the kid wear it! Sure! Cut it down when the time came. A smelly hand-me-down, whether the kid liked it or not!"[7] Eli too has become a conscious pariah.

The exploration of the conditions of character is central to these novels. The effect is that of individuals at odds with their circumstances; harmony with their environment is not possible, but while possessing the energy to transform it, the realities are such that only small changes are possible. Thus these characters respond to the world from which they emerge by a stubborn unwillingness to be coopted by their surroundings. One of the strongest possible models for their lives is that of the pícaro, the rogue, a form developed by critical Jewish thinkers, new Christians, caught in the confines of Catholic Spain. As Thomas Edwards notes in a review of Bashevis Singer's *Enemies, a Love Story*, the pícaro is determined to invent his own life; through deceit he fabricates for himself a counter-reality. Ben Siegel calls them confidence men: "each is either more than he appears or less."[8] The measure of their mysteriousness is their ability to stand up to the world and then have enough wit to deceive it.

They interfere with the world's expectations because they will not relinquish the sources of their native value. This is also the cause of their strength of character. The project of inventing one's own life is part and parcel of the modern enterprise; the habit of using deceit in order to fabricate a counter-reality in which to function derives from an understanding of the limits within which the pícaro is expected to devise his own life. He too can exist as a human being so long as he gives up the habit of being a Jew. Deceit, then, is his weapon, appearance his strategy in smuggling into a narrow reality the full range of his humanity. It is a project that breeds cynicism and even has nihilistic possibilities; it is also one that has very little chance of being stopped. Emancipation has loosed messianic energies that propel the Jew through his new world.

This is not a project limited to Jewish men, of course. Bashevis Singer and Philip Roth include as their subject the effect of emancipation on Jewish women. Released from the confines of the shtetl, the Jewish woman emerges in all her strength—as mother, wife, and lover. Like her male counterpart, she is a mystery to herself and to those around her. Here is a typical exchange in a recent story by Singer:

> One good trait she did have—she could attract a man. Sexually, she was amazingly strong. I don't believe myself that I am speaking of these things—in my circles, talk of sex is taboo. But why? . . . She has a powerful imagination, a perverse fantasy. I've had experience with women and I know. She has said things to me that drove me to frenzy. She has more stories in her than Scheherezade. Our days were cursed, but the nights were wild. She wore me out until I could no longer do my work . . . I have the feeling that many Jewish women in Poland are of this type. I see it in their eyes . . . I have a theory that the Jewish woman of today wants to make up for all the centuries in the ghetto. Besides, the Jews are a people of imagination.[9]

The last phrase echoes Hannah Arendt's: the conscious pariah liberates himself through the force of the imagination. Like this woman in Singer's story, the pariah invents an ideal of freedom that she comes to embody, in effect, bringing into being that plural possibility of full emancipation for all. We hear an echo of the project of those Spanish writers who filled their fictional worlds with pícaros so that in the real world there might be the hoped-for possibility of a *convivencia*, a living together of Jew, Christian, and Moslem.

As we have seen, the problematics of Jewish identity in the

modern world receive careful scrutiny in these writings and are constantly linked to clothing. Between appearance and reality, there is the mysterious self of these characters that serves as a clotheshorse and, as well, a bundle of contradictions.

If Sholom Aleichem focuses the fantasy, the benefit, and the cost of passing for a gentile, even a "Buttons" (his nickname for a Russian official whose uniform was resplendent with gold braid), in the transformative power of a hat, then Bashevis Singer expresses the value of tradition in shoes and shoemaking. For Singer, the house of the little shoemakers—crumbling, moldy, held up by a prayer—embodies tradition, but it is shoemaking that truly puts those values into action in daily life. The stories of these two Yiddish masters enable us to comprehend one crucial aspect of the remaking of Jewish tradition and life that occurs when the Jew is seduced and propelled out of the shtetl into the modern world.

In both "On Account of a Hat" and "The Little Shoemakers," clothing assumes the status of a code that parallels the other semiotic systems of social reality. There is more than one kind of clothing, and society is divided into two different kinds of clothes users, Jewish or Gentile. To appropriate the clothing of one and wear it in the other situation implies the desire to appear different from what one is. The lives of the characters of these stories are carefully circumscribed. Each is set within his own realm, so that to cross into the other is not to be done easily or consciously. In both stories the moment of transition from the Jewish to the non-Jewish realm takes place in the circumstances of a dream. In Sholom Aleichem's story, the protagonist mistakenly puts on the hat of a government official as he is awakened to catch an early morning train. Because of his new hat, he receives official treatment: the line at the ticket window melts away before him, the porter takes his bag, and he is ushered into the first-class railway car.

Looking in the mirror, he experiences an identity crisis: "Maybe he's dreaming. Sholem Shachnah rubs his forehead, and while passing down the corridor glances into the mirror on the wall. It nearly knocks him over. He sees not himself but the official with the red band. That's who it is!" His unexpected good fortune and his successful though unwitting impersonation is not something Sholem Shachnah can account for. The comedy of the story results from his assertion of his Jewish self as his unitary identity. "Twenty times I tell him [the porter] to wake me and I even give him a tip, and what does he do, that dumb ox, may he catch cholera in his face, but wake the official instead. And me he leaves asleep on the bench!"[10]

Farcical humor concludes the identity-crisis episode: "Now get a load of this. Sholem Shachnah scoops up his carpetbag and rushes off once more, right back to the station where he is sleeping on the bench. He's going to wake himself up before the locomotive, God forbid, lets out a blast." He cannot accept the good fortune of even momentarily being someone he isn't; his reward is the misfortune of being only and always who he is. He is from now on taunted in Kasrilevke for his unconscious desires and his conscious failures: "They pointed him out in the streets and held their sides, laughing. And everybody asked him, 'How does it feel, Reb Sholem Shachnah, to wear a cap with a red band and a visor.' 'And tell us,' said others, 'what's it like to travel first class?' As for the children, this was made to order for them—you hear what I say? Wherever he went they trooped after him, shouting, 'Your Excellency! Your excellent Excellency! Your most excellent Excellency!' "[11]

Sholem Shachnah's momentary dream vision becomes in Bashevis Singer's "The Little Shoemakers" Abba Shuster's extended nightmare. Neither of the two protagonists really wants to cross the boundary into the non-Jewish world, and neither desires a new identity. Yet both heroes have to cope with the fact of a new self, occasioned by the new clothing they are forced to wear. For Abba, leaving his home does not come easily; it is the Nazi invasion of Poland that forces him off. Like Sholem Shachnah, Abba also has great difficulty in accounting for this new experience. He interprets the attack of the dive bombers and the noise of the artillery as the onset of the messianic era. In the course of his wanderings, he loses his shoemaker's tools as well as his prayer shawl and tefillin; like Sholem Shachnah, he has lost his identity.

All of this takes place in what for Abba is a nightmarish Armageddon. There are no separate events to mark the undifferentiated flow of time; he loses count of the days and so cannot celebrate the Sabbath; he does not know if the food he is offered is kosher and so subsists on bread and water. He undergoes death and rebirth, as the universe is reconstituted before his eyes. "During the day Abba kept watch at the porthole over his bunk. The ship would leap up as if mounting the sky, and the torn sky would fall as though the world were returning to original chaos. Then the ship would plunge back into the ocean, and once again the firmament would be divided from the waters, as in the Book of Genesis. The waves were a sulphurous yellow and black. Now they would sawtooth out to the horizon like a mountain range, reminding Abba of the Psalmist's words: 'The mountains skipped like rams, the little hills like lambs.' Then they would come heaving back, as in the miraculous Parting of the Waters." Distinctions are no longer possible for him. All the biblical stories merge into a model by which to interpret his own life. "Abba had little learning, but Biblical references ran through his mind, and he saw himself as the Prophet Jonah, who fled before God. He too lay in the belly of a whale and, like Jonah, prayed to God for deliverance. Then it would seem to him that this was not ocean but limitless desert, crawling with serpents, monsters, and dragons, as it is written in Deuteronomy." The reality of his situation includes his beliefs as well as his physical state. "He hardly slept a wink at night. When he got up to relieve himself, he would feel faint and lose his balance. With great difficulty he would regain his feet and, his knees buckling under, go wandering, lost, down the narrow, winding corridor, groaning and calling for help until a sailor led him back to the cabin. Whenever this happened he was sure that he was dying. He would not even receive decent Jewish burial but be dumped in the ocean. And he made his confession, beating his knotty fist on his chest and exclaiming, 'Forgive me, Father!' "[12] His strength lies in being unable to separate his Jewish habits from his modern situation.

What in Sholom Aleichem's story is a momentary identity crisis becomes in Bashevis Singer's story a transition from the settled world of Frampol, with its respect for the artisan and its traditional rabbinic Judaism, to modern America with its unfamiliar Judaism and mechanized technology. Abba believes he is leaving the world of tradition and Judaism for the wanderings of the Bible. He is not a learned man, but he has a vivid imagination that helps him to construe his journey in the terms of the patriarchs' experience. When he is reunited with his sons in Elizabeth, New Jersey, he responds to the experience by weaving together the moments of recognition of Joseph, his brothers, and Jacob:

> The old man closed his eyes and made no answer. Their voices ran together, everything was turning pell-mell, topsy-turvy. Suddenly he thought of Jacob arriving in Egypt, where he was met by Pharoah's chariots. He felt he had lived through the same experience in a previous incarnation. His beard began to tremble, a hoarse sob rose from his chest. A forgotten passage from the Bible stuck in his gullet.
>
> Blindly he embraced one of his sons and sobbed out, "Is this you? Alive?"
>
> He had meant to say: "Now let me die, since I have seen thy face, because thou art yet alive."[13]

Abba's strength lies in his ability to project himself into the sacred books of his culture and through them make sense of confusing modern values. His weakness as a father is due to his inability to comprehend the desires of his sons for something besides the traditional routine and daily ritual of the grubby shtetl of Frampol. In the encounter between his eldest son and Abba, Singer has presented the confrontation between modernity and tradition and shown how incomprehensible each is to the other.

> The boy spoke up, but Abba couldn't understand a word of it. He laid into synagogue and state with such venom, Abba could only imagine that the poor soul was possessed: the Hebrew teachers beat the children, the women empty their slop pails right outside the door, the shopkeepers loiter in the streets, there are no toilets anywhere and the public relieves itself as it pleases, behind the bathhouse or out in the open, encouraging epidemics and plagues. He made fun of Ezreal the healer and of Mecheles the marriage

broker, nor did he spare the rabbinical court and the bath
attendant, the washerwoman and the overseer of the poor-
house, the professions and the benevolent societies.

Abba's response is clear: "At first Abba was afraid that the boy
had lost his mind, but the longer he continued his harangue, the
clearer it became that he had strayed from the path of righteous-
ness." The values of tradition are incomprehensible to the modern, and yet the two are inextricable and, like Abba and his
sons, will have to live together. Tradition is the reference point
of modernity, as hand-crafted shoes are the standard against
which the Shusters measure their mass production of shoes—a
theme caught in the humorous phrasing of the advertisement by
which the brothers proclaim their modern link to tradition.
"Our experience dates back three hundred years to the Polish
city of Brod, where our ancestor, Abba, learned the craft from a
local master. The community of Frampol, in which our family
worked at its trade for fifteen generations, bestowed on him the
title of Master in recognition of his charitable services. This
sense of public responsibility has always gone hand in hand
with our devotion to the highest principles of the craft and our
strict policy of honest dealing with our customers."[14]
Abba the shoemaker lives a unified life in Frampol. His work
and his life are one; he continues the traditions of his fathers in
work as well as in ritual. He too makes seven pairs of shoes for
the orphans of the town every year; he too names his sons after
dead forebears so that their names may continue. Tradition is
unbroken: shoemaking is an analogue to the transmission of the
Torah from generation to generation. Bashevis Singer focuses
both in his use of the Yiddish word *arbeit* for the shoemaking
activity, a German loan word. For most Yiddish readers, the
context of work as worship established in the story makes it an
activity that easily translates into the Hebrew word *avodah*,
with its connotations of religious service and worship.[15]
Frampol is a coherent and meaningful world. Abba sees in his
mouldering house not a decaying building but the layers of
tradition.

Evenings, when the sun was setting, the house would be
pervaded by a dusky glow. Rays of light danced in the

corners, flicked across the ceiling, and set Abba's beard gleaming with the color of spun gold. Pesha, Abba's wife, would be cooking *kasha* and soup in the kitchen, the children would be playing, neighboring women and girls would go in and out of the house. Abba would rise from his work, wash his hands, put on his long coat, and go off to the tailors' synagogue for evening prayers. He knew that the wide world was full of strange cities and distant lands, that Frampol was actually no bigger than a dot in a small prayer book; but it seemed to him that his little town was the navel of the universe and that his own house stood at the very center.

In its very coherence, Frampol deceives Abba into imagining it to be the center of the universe. "He often thought that when the Messiah came to lead the Jews to the land of Israel, he, Abba, would stay behind in Frampol, in his own house, on his own hill. Only on the Sabbath and on Holy Days would he step into a cloud and let himself be flown to Jerusalem."[16] Living according to rabbinic tradition and Talmudic law, Abba yet moves in a fairy-tale world. In Frampol, there is room for neither past history nor modern experience, and Abba will have to leave it. In his nakedness, he will have to confront the terror of history, which will appear with biblical force to someone whose experience of history, modernity, and terror have previously been restricted to his meditations on the good book.

"The Little Shoemakers" is a story that juxtaposes two frames of reference. In it Frampol is a fairy-tale world, with Abba, his ancestors, and his children as the seven dwarfs of legend. Outside this shtetl we encounter a biblical realm where man is naked before history because he, the center of all contradictions, participates in it. His character brings on that terror as well, as he discovers the possibility of transcendence in history, perhaps making possible some sort of redemption. But "The Little Shoemakers" evades generic resolution and ends ambiguously, even sweetly. Abba is reconciled with his children, who have become shoe manufacturers in New Jersey, by virtue of the secret knowledge he imparted to them in Frampol. At the end of the story, father and sons wield their craft once more and sing their jingle of tradition.

Abba raised his dense eyebrows, and his sad eyes looked around at his heirs, the seven shoemakers: Gimpel, Getzel, Treitel, Godel, Feivel, Lippe, and Chananiah. Their hair was white, though yellow streaks remained. No, praise God, they had not become idolaters in Egypt. They had not forgotten their heritage, nor had they lost themeselves among the unworthy. The old man rattled and bumbled deep in his chest, and suddenly began to sing in a stifled, hoarse voice:

> "A mother had
> Ten little boys,
> Oh, Lord, ten little boys!
> The sixth one was called Velvele,
> The seventh one was called Zeinvele,
> The eighth one was called Chenele,
> The ninth one was called Tevele,
> The tenth one was called Judele . . ."

And Abba's sons came in on the chorus:

> "Oh, Lord, Judele!"[17]

Abba never confronts the urban experience in momentarily reconstituting his shtetl in New Jersey. It is only in his novels of urban life that Singer's characters encounter the splintering of personality and the modern separation of roles from functions. It is in Warsaw or New York that such characters struggle to discover who they are. Like Herman Broder, who is "a riddle to himself," they engage in a quest for self-knowledge in which the modern city is the arena and stage for the self's repertory of seemingly unrelated roles and meanings.[18]

The attention paid to the body in *Enemies*, the endless fascination with its different parts dressed and undressed, is an analogue to the delight Singer shares with Henry Roth in describing the different neighborhoods of this gargantuan city. In attending to the city's diversity, we pay attention to the potential for different selves each of these characters has. With a plot that forces the novel's protagonist to embed his life in an increasingly intricate network of lies and then confront his different roles, past histories and present fabrications, we come to read in the city a geography of the self.

The urban world is one of appearance. At moments of crisis, Herman wishes he were wearing his good suit. He is taunted by his inability to be properly dressed: "All these women you could find, and your coat you can't find?" Despite Herman's effort to discover who he really is, he fails to evoke an image of himself; his passionate lovemaking and musing with his mistress Masha, is an effort to uncover their identities. Taking off their clothes or putting them on, they uncover not real expressions of their selves but layers of selfhood, with nothing but a question mark at the center, Levinsky's situation once more. It is significant that Masha makes her own clothes, creating an image out of outworn hand-me-downs, which make her always the glamorous, dramatic center of the scene. Always choosing who she will be and what role she will play, she is the apotheosis of the modern Jewish woman. Nevertheless, the novel unravels lives and lies, until Herman realizes, "She has no more control over her actions than I have over mine," as he reflects upon their characters almost at the end of the novel, just before she commits suicide.[19]

Masha is the freethinker of this novel, Herman the pícaro, but neither has a self as Abba does. Herman, ghost writer for a rabbinical parvenu, fails to devise roles for himself through his writing. When he is occasionally jolted out of his frenzied urban rush into attending to the traditional words of the Talmud, he enters the world that Abba cherishes. At that moment, Herman is drawn to repentance; he glimpses the possibility of self-order in the ancient roles. Just as quickly, Herman finds himself pulled back into the effort to cover up his shame.

Like David Schearl, Herman cannot live in Abba's fairy tale; both inhabit a realm much closer to that of the biblical narratives, where they must confront the terror of history and selfhood in search of redemption. David's act of calling up power from the earth parallels Isaiah's, while perhaps reversing the sources of power. Herman decides to leave and thereby reaffirm his roguishness, like a Yiddish Augie March. He is committed to the border crossing, making it his cosmic theory of survival, a fit world view for the Holocaust survivor.

> In Herman's private philosophy, survival itself was based on guile. From microbe to man, life prevailed gener-

ation to generation by sneaking past the jealous powers of destruction. Just like the Tzivkever smugglers in World War I, who stuffed their boots and blouses with tobacco, secreted all manner of contraband about their bodies, and stole across borders, breaking laws and bribing officials— so did every bit of protoplasm, or conglomerate of protoplasm furtively traffic its way from epoch to epoch. It had been so when the first bacteria appeared in the slime at the ocean's edge and would be so when the sun became a cinder and the last living creature on earth froze to death, or perished in whichever way the final biological drama dictated. Animals had accepted the precariousness of existence and the necessity for flight and stealth; only man sought certainty and instead succeeded in accomplishing his own downfall. The Jew had always managed to smuggle his way in through crime and madness. He had stolen into Canaan and into Egypt. Abraham had pretended that Sarah was his sister. The whole two thousand years of exile, beginning with Alexandria, Babylon, and Rome and ending in the ghettos of Warsaw, Lodz, and Vilna had been one great act of smuggling. The Bible, the Talmud, and the Commentaries instruct the Jew in one strategy: flee from evil, hide from danger, avoid showdowns, give the angry powers of the universe as wide a berth as possible. The Jew never looked askance at the deserter who crept into a cellar or attic while armies clashed in the streets outside.

Herman, the modern Jew, had extended this principle one step; he no longer even had his faith in the Torah to depend on. He was deceiving not only Abimelech but Sarah and Hagar as well.[20]

Selfhood is the secret of this world and its scandal, individuation its theme and central concern. Here the preoccupation of modern Jewish writers links up with that of Hawthorne and Melville who in Hester Prynne, Young Goodman Brown, Ahab, and Ishmael also founded their theory of character on scandal and secrecy. For in the traditional worlds from which these writers emerge, to have a self and be an individual with the capacity to choose is reason enough for expulsion from the communal garden.

Ashamed of themselves because like Adam and Eve they have partaken of the forbidden fruit, these characters recognize their nakedness and in that moment seek to cover it with leaves. In the Yiddish version of this passage from Genesis 3:6-7, the word for leaves is also used, as in English, for pages—a pun suggesting the many uses of knowledge in the modern world: "Had they [not] eaten from the tree of knowledge, they would have gone about naked, without clothes, and would not have been ashamed. But since they ate from the fruit of the tree they became ashamed of themselves, and tore off leaves to cover their shame." Covering themselves with the clothing of their now various roles, they assert their existence as characters in the same gestures used to hide it. As well, these gestures hide and reveal the subtext of tradition that informs these modern works.

4
Abishag: The Body's Song

Perhaps we can account for the ease with which biblical figures appear in Yiddish poetry by the enduring Jewish habit of translation, which was so often brought into play in order to make holy writ available to unlettered folk. We know of many Yiddish versions of the Bible, preceding Yiddish poetry by several hundred years, that helped to shape the idiom before it was perfected by its writers. What is harder to comprehend is the way in which the heroes and heroines of the sacred Hebrew were transformed into the village dwellers of the mother tongue. In Yiddish poetry, David, Rachel, Naomi, Ruth, and Elijah are not ancient mythic actors; nor are they the protagonists of historical narratives and lyrics who, despite their temporal distance, pronounce stern judgment on an unheroic present, as is the case in so much of modern Hebrew literature. Especially in the poetry of Itzik Manger, they inhabit the everyday world of the shtetl and the modern town in an eternally recurring present. The biblical qualities of their spirit are as it were immanent in the texture and daily life of the folk—that is, in their language's subtle mixture of the holy tongue, in which these heroic figures first made an appearance, and the secular linguistic realms of German and Polish, which added a mundane vocabulary and an analytic syntax to the prophetic strains and inflected structure of Hebrew and thus produced the triumph that is Yiddish.

Flexible, supple, witty, ironic, and playful, its ability to be conscious of its peculiar status as a special language, echoing in its very texture the precarious amalgam of European Jewish life, reaches a remarkable intensity when it deals with biblical figures: it is as if the Hebrew letters in which it is written reveal its biblical characteristics even in an adopted vocabulary. Surely such a notion lies behind the declaration of the introspectivists of modern Yiddish poetry who, led by Jacob Glatstein, showed how any subject could be Jewish if it were but dealt with in this Yiddish tongue. And the irony and paradox of the culture articulated by the mother tongue of western Jewry compels our attention when we encounter its narrative of biblical events told by characters who, notably in Manger's poetry, have read the sacred account that includes their lives.

In the very texture of their language these writers confront the general problems of imaginative writing in the modern world, exploring them with a personal, unique, and brilliant intensity. Their poetry echoes the long tradition of biblical and postbiblical Hebrew lyricism, stakes out its own territory in modern Western literature, culminating in an unusually wide range that encompasses folk and high culture. Thus many of their poems are sung in the street as ballads and yet can enter the consciousness of a people as if they were psalms of a contemporary David, functioning even as prayers in a contemporary, skeptical, bitter mode dedicated to the service of an ancient God.[1]

To look through the intense lenses of Yiddish poetry at Abishag, who makes her brief appearance, in I Kings 1:1-4, 15, as David's substitute for an electric blanket, is to observe the encounter of the world-historical Jewish king, conqueror of Jerusalem and founder of it as capital of all the Jews, and the *pintele yid*, the anonymous Jew, who makes up the substratum of Jewish life so often unreflected in its national consciousness. The meeting of the two—great king and little woman at his service—marks out the area Yiddish literature made its own. How interesting then to find in Glatstein's poem as well as Manger's Abishag group an encounter between two speakers on a not so unequal level.

Manger's Abishag knows—because she has read her story in the Bible—that for her deeds she will only receive "a shura in Tanach," a line in the Bible:

> A line for her young flesh,
> the years of her youth.
> A line of ink on parchment
> for the whole long truth,

as Ruth Whitman so finely translates the bittersweet lament.[2] Abishag speaks out in her sleep in the previous poem of Manger's cycle of all those village things she has left behind in coming to the court.

> Abishag sleeps. She breathes quietly.
> But listen—in her sleep she speaks,
> and from her dream she breathes
> the scent of calves and sheep.

Having put aside his book of psalms, which he has been wearily thumbing, King David approaches her bed. He overhears her dream speech, and the heroic lutanist hearkens to her village world, of

> A pond, a pine forest,
> a giant village moon,
> an old and pious linden tree
> that watches over mama's house.

Abishag's entranced evocation of the natural world echoes the characteristic Wordsworthian process by which we make nature into our lasting spiritual home. In the previous poem it has bestowed remarkable gifts on her. Even at the moment of her departure from this natural realm,

> the weary sun at evening
> adds to her summer dress
> a great and golden blossom.

But now in the king's bedroom, Abishag's sleepy words carry

> a sad and haunting tone,
> homesickness that draws the king
> from his psalter and becomes
> its own song.

This is a superb lyric moment in which the full contrast between David and Abishag flashes upon us. It is also the moment of

Abishag's triumph, in her simplicity and naturalness, over the world of the court and the city. Her body, which according to the story is to be used only to warm the great king, her youthful being that is to be demeaned into an instrument asserts its value as body, in making a song of her native realm. By this song she asserts her right to be, even in David's presence.

Manger's poem ends as the old and weary king kisses Abishag and withdraws.

> He bends the old white head,
> kissing the village-life in her,
> kissing the old linden tree
> that watches over her mother's door.

Sighing, stroking his beard, David returns to his loneliness and his ancient psalms, thumbing through his psalter. Separated from her by his age, piety, and sophistication, David, the sweet singer of Israel, here accepts and thus legitimates her world, with his gesture marking and recognizing Abishag's integrity and intrinsic value. The young girl has enacted an ironic Cinderella story, leaving a humble hearth for the great modern world of a king,

> whose portrait
> hangs for years now on the wall
> above her mother's bed.

She expects him to be

> the prince of her dreams,
> young and slender,

and in her excitement of anticipation has imagined herself a fancy lady. Yet she lives through the saddening tale of modern Jewish life in a poem that is not only a criticism of the false allure of the modern world but a comment on urbanization's inevitable effect on simple folk. David's kiss enshrines the value of her transitory village realm. The mighty one has stooped to the humble, the simple girl has spoken to the great king and been hearkened to, the nation has been made whole.

Manger's final poem in the cycle, in which Abishag is figured as writing a sad letter home, describing her life with old and pious King David,

and she herself is "oh, well"—
She's the king's hotwater bottle
against the bedroom chill,

concludes with the ironic promise of a line in the Bible as recompense for her young life. In characteristic fashion, Manger trans-
figures this seemingly petty reward of posterity by evoking the
human meanings from which it grows.

Abishag puts down her pen,
her heart is strangely bitter,
a tear drips from her eyes
and falls on the letter.

The tear erases "mother"
and erases "linden tree"
while girlish in a corner
a dream sobs tenderly.

In focusing his poetic cycle on her, Manger rescues Abishag
from her subservient position in the David chronicle. Endowing
her with multiple value in having her enact the trajectory of
modern Jewish life, he transforms her into a symbolic figure
powerfully expressing—as she lives through it—the predica-
ment of the modern Jew. The king she serves, whose portrait
hangs above her mother's bed, might be Franz Joseph of Austria
as well as David of Israel; and she is every village girl who, having left home for the urban possibilities of the modern city,
writes home in acknowledgment of the spiritual cost of her journey. Rooted in the biblical tale, she takes on in Manger's poems
the Chagallian coloration of the shtetl faced with its disintegra-
tion before the force of the modern world.

As the modest and simple girl, Manger's Abishag does not reflect the limited yet significant and even heroic role the rabbis
assigned to her in Jewish tradition. In the Talmud she receives
several lines of bemused conversation, all in all the glory of a
paragraph of rabbinical discussion emphasizing her holiness
and devotion, in linking her to another woman of Shunem,
whose hospitable welcome of the prophet Elisha brought her
praise and succor. In Jewish tradition she is ancillary to David,
and when Adonijah wants to marry her after David's death, the

rabbis approve of Solomon's decision to eliminate his half-brother's feeble-hearted claim for the Davidic role in denying him her hand.[3] Manger's achievement then is to rescue Abishag from a kingly tale by making her the representative of the folk on whose backs the royal pyramid of power and authority, be it David's or Franz Joseph's, rests. As she sleepily creates her own song out of memories of her village world, Abishag speaks for its creative energy and vitality, that makes a world out of the simplest elements of nature, home, and hearth. Abishag thus becomes a figure of basic human value, unlimited to her ethnic role in an ancient Hebrew story—an evocation of the natural energy and warmth of humankind.

The relationship between David and Abishag is striking, echoing deep male desires on a psychic level and the actual diminution of woman into man's servant in so much of human history. Compared to other facets of the David story, notable for the imaginative riches with which succeeding generations have elaborated them, the encounter of David and Abishag is almost untouched. Jewish tradition is relatively silent on the subject, as if the rabbis had sought to repress a particularly dangerous issue in refusing to explore it. By contrast, Manger and Glatstein bring the question of the place of women in Jewish life to a sharp focus in their poems, allowing us to consider its many aspects while focusing on its sexual center.

The Abishag poems make reference to a famous literary topos of western non-Jewish culture, that of the *senex amans*. In their silence on the subject, the rabbis suggest the extent of their embarassment at what the biblical story includes in a matter-of-fact way as part of the history of the Davidic era. Both Manger's and Glatstein's poems echo the biblical account. Unlike Boccaccio's senescent males or Chaucer's January lusting after May, the Yiddish writers depict a *senex amans* despite himself. Though Abishag ministers to David and cares for him, the old king—in that consistent biblical phrase linking sexuality, self-consciousness, and knowledge—"knew her not."

The failure of David's masculinity is an apt prelude in the biblical account to the effort of Adonijah to declare himself king, an action that rouses David to declare Solomon his true heir, as the narrator chronicles the political intrigues of a patri-

archal society. In such a world, the power of maleness is the
necessary condition for kingly rule, its absence the sign that the
crown must pass to a younger, more virile heir. In the poems of
Manger and Glatstein David's impotence takes on a personal
rather than social value, which enables them to consider Abishag's role in the relationship, rather than passing over it as do
the David chronicles.

In treating the relationship of Abishag and David, Manger
and Glatstein bring the concerns of nature, the body, and sexuality to a literary tradition notable for the absence of these
themes. It is enough for us to recall the peculiar linguistic energy
of Sholom Aleichem's world, where speech is a surrogate for
nature and the bodily passions, prosaic social experience pre-
dominates, and the institutional life of the Jews is so wittily rep-
resented, to comprehend the force of the Abishag poems. In
effect, Manger and Glatstein figure for us a world in which
speech can become song because it expresses the longings and
meanings of the body. In Manger's world we have the evocation
of these possibilities through their dialectic negation, com-
pressed into a stanza of Abishag's letter:

> Greet the handsome miller
> who works in the mill—
> and the shepherd Oizer, whose
> piping she cherishes still,

she writes home to her mother. It is the miracle of his poetry
that from the absence of bodily and spiritual fulfillment Manger
can evoke for us its potential promise. For him, as for Bashevis
Singer—notably in his novel *The Slave*—it is the body's song
that is supreme, possible only when enacted among equals and
unavailable to either man or woman when the power of lust and
the lust of power degrades man into master and woman into
slave. Transforming Abishag into David's equal by allowing
her the right of speech, Manger cuts through the sexist knot.

For the vehicle of encounter between old king and young
maiden in Manger's and Glatstein's poems is their mutual ability to speak to each other—an ancient and powerful vision of
the deepest force of language as metaphoric and even actual sexual intercourse. As he evokes this image out of their meeting,

Manger encompasses the widest possible human experience and symbolically focuses the multiple possibilities for human self-realization within the nation's realm. Part of the power of his images grows out of the social and chronological inequalities that are overcome when the old king and the young maiden respond to each other by allowing their basic human concerns the space in which to be articulated.

In Glatstein's poem,[4] Abishag becomes David's equal in a more intense way, focused even more closely on the links between sexuality and language than Manger's. Here too we have an old king, who calls to her in longing. For him she is "Abishag. Little, youthful, warm Abishag." But now David feels himself close to death, and Abishag comforts him through his long night of despair. Glatstein's poem compresses David's career into a few remarkable and intense lines: the people in the streets will not let him sleep. As he calls out in despair at the bands of Adonijah's supporters who demand the throne for the son, though his old father yet lives, Abishag soothes him. For David, she is the only servant left, as the others all jockey for the succession. Even Bat-Sheva, his beloved,

> Fat Bat-Sheva blesses me with eternal life and with
> a sly smile watches for my last words.

An antiphonal, strophic dialogue, the poem echoes the great biblical lyrics in its poetic structure and its free verse. It recounts Abishag's steadfastness as she responds ever more strongly to David's increasingly bitter strictures. At first he tells her, "Cry out into the street: King David has not yet died!" A stanza later he is ready to relinquish the throne:

> Throw my crown into the street, and let whoever
> wants to catch it!

But as his bitterness grows, Abishag answers him by subtly varying her declaration of loyalty suffused with love. First she soothes him:

> Sleep, my King. The night is dead. We are all your
> faithful servants.

Then as his hysteria increases, she answers his strident queries,

> Nap, my King. The night is still. We are all your
>   faithful servants.

Glatstein's masterful variation of the refrain, one of the characteristics of his finest poems, is striking.

> Rest, my King. The night is still. We are all your
>   faithful servants,

Abishag says. And later she tells him to dream, concluding the poem.

> Sleep deeply, my King. Day will soon dawn. We are all your
>   faithful servants.

Here I think Glatstein captures certain essential qualities of the biblical account. We recognize that David is king because songs were sung by and of him. His legitimacy results not only from the power of his sword but the truth of his words. We participate in David's act of remembering the force of those words in the agony of old age, when the memories of triumphs that evoke past glories congeal like blood.

It is his power with words and the power of his figure in words that has made him king. He is the poet of Israel whose singing surges from his being in its commitment to God and people. David reaches out to understand his career, as poet, warrior, and king, calling out to Abishag in one of the climactic lines of the poem: "Abishag, surely songs are truer than sin," as he longs to believe the psalms of his pious youth will stand witness for him at the final judgment.

Glatstein's poem articulates the encounter between David and Abishag through a profound appreciation of the sexual basis of language. Though their consummation is physically impossible, on the level of speech—an older generation would say, on a spiritual plane—it is accomplished. In the playfulness and seriousness with which they respond to each other's words, we have almost a model of sexual encounter. The teasing epithets with which David endows Abishag are echoed by the changing refrain with which she answers him, constantly deflecting his attention from his distress, perhaps in order to keep him from letting his wit and consciousness of himself as impotent and senescent lover turn into self-pity. She leads him to a spiritual realization, as he exclaims over the power of song to outface sin itself and overcome the horrors of the wars in which he has engaged.

For a moment we are reminded in this poem, as we are in Manger's, that David the warrior, able even in old age to overcome the incipient rebellion of Adonijah, also has a feminine side—that of the youthful singer and lover of Jonathan. Glatstein's poem manifests the power of song, echoing David's traditional achievement as the composer of the Book of Psalms, and suggests that it is in David's ability to unite masculine as well as feminine attributes that his enduring value consists.

The past glories of his song are countered here—at the same moment they are evoked—in Abishag's singing, for now the village maiden from Shunem sings to David as she rocks him to sleep in a song at once lullaby and pledge of fealty. She is his only servant, his singer and solace, and it is nothing more than her song emanating from the warmth and youth of her being that staves off the death David cries out against. Paradoxically, then, Abishag plays the healing role parallel to that which David, the young lutanist from rural Bethlehem, enacted for King Saul.

For both Abishag and David, poetry is God's gift and brings health and life. Their song encompasses the sad tale of war and politics and transforms it. This bodily speech is not only an artistic creation but a procreative one. It articulates the poet's being and the nation's existence, as in Glatstein's remarkable technical feat it assures him of life at the very edge of death. Thereby his poem enacts the situation of the post-Holocaust Yiddish poet, writing in a tongue that resurrects and gives life to a world most brutally exterminated; and yet because of his poetic act of witness and reenactment, it is unvanquished.

In the most interesting modern European versions of biblical tales, Abishag is not a conspicuous figure. Thomas Mann's magisterial retelling of the Joseph story does not of course include her, nor does she appear in Dan Jacobson's *The Rape of Tamar*, but she is given a poem in two short sections early in the first part of Rilke's *Neue Gedichte*. This relatively little-known lyric is part of an early biblical group in the collection. "David

Singt Vor Saul" and "Josuas Landtag" come immediately after, violating chronology but developing Rilke's thematic concern with the relation of singing, poetry, and knowledge. Abishag also appears in Gladys Schmitt's brilliant novel *David, the King* and serves there to focus similar themes.[5]

In Rilke's poem as well as Schmitt's novel, Abishag plays a mythic role. The young girl involved with the ancient king of Israel, enacts in both works a metaphysical even theologically centered role through her physical caring for David. Schmitt recaptures the heroic qualities of the original; her portrait of Abishag has many affinities with Glatstein's poem. By contrast, stressing the extraordinary qualities of the encounter, Rilke reaches for different effects.

His poem does not contextualize Abishag's figure in her village world, as do the other versions; more abstract, it does not locate Abishag within an easily apprehended mundane world as do Manger's witty and playful poems. Rilke's poem—unlike Manger's, Glatstein's, and Schmitt's novel—does not give her the right of personal speech. Rather, she serves as the occasion for a profound meditation on themes that reach apotheosis in some of the more famous poems of the *Neue Gedichte*, "Apollo: Archaic Torso" or "Orpheus, Eurydice, Hermes." Nevertheless, here too we find the remarkable sculptural insight into the intersection of corporeality and spirituality that characterize his greater poems.

For Rilke, the encounter of David and Abishag becomes a symbol of unfulfillment. If she is aching youth, he is immobilized age. Though they meet each other only in the dark, her night is bright and lit by stars while his is cold and unilluminated. David cannot respond to her "unstirred mouth that cannot kiss," even though he is "skilled in the knowledge of women." The poem plays variations on an image from the preceding one, "Eastern Aubade," and figures their meeting in terms of a natural scene of desolation.

> But at evening Abishag arched
> over him. His mazy being lay
> abandoned like the coastline of an infamous ocean
> beneath the constellation of her quiet breasts.

He is an isolated coast unable to respond to the call of her star. Three lines later, the roles reverse and

> the green wand of her feelings
> did not incline to his ground.
> He shivered.

Though Rilke associates David and Abishag by means of these images with the fertility encounters of heaven and earth common to Babylonian lore, he also reveals their inability to play the traditional fructifying mythic roles. The gap between her youth and his age is too great for knowledge—sexual or cosmic —and the poem leaves them isolated each within an appointed realm.

In turning to anthropomorphic images, Rilke clearly shows the difference between his interest in Abishag and David and the concerns of Manger and Glatstein. For the Yiddish poets such anthropomorphism is blasphemous, steeped as they are in an iconoclastic tradition. To suggest that David and Abishag play transhuman roles and enact a shadowy version of the encounter of earth and heaven is to deprive them of their human freedom. According to Jewish tradition, the human being is in history and therefore able to perform his own destiny precisely because he is not bound to enact and reiterate the encounters of the gods. Banishing the pagan idols, he no longer accepts their limitations as rules for his life, but instead is freed to order the world and thereby realize his true nature in making use of the divine power with which he has been endowed by virtue of creation in the divine image. According to very old traditions, central to both Jewish and Christian thought, it is speech— logos, the word—that incarnates the human being's divinely granted power.

It is the inability of Rilke's figures to make contact with each other that is the central theme of his poem. Their frustrated striving for a meaningful and self-conscious relation—sexual as well as linguistic, two realms that are so often metaphorically intertwined—parallels Rilke's often desperate effort in the *Neue Gedichte* to bring Greek and Hebrew traditions into vital encounter, out of which alone he feels can come the fructifying speech he seeks. In "Abisag" Rilke enacts the effort to transform

the gods of myth into human figures and thereby marry ancient
hellenistic values and the prophetic speech of the Hebrew Bible.
As Rilke brings these two cultures together in the *Neue Gedichte*
we are reminded of the similar efforts of Franz Rosenzweig and
Martin Buber, which occurred at roughly the same time, to
bring into being in their Free Jewish House of Study at Frankfort
as well as their translation of the Bible into German, a similar
cultural confrontation that would reveal the elements from
which the biblical synthesis emerged. Though Manger may
have met Rilke, and is recorded as having been envious of his
fame,[6] his concern like Glatstein's was to domesticate Abishag
and David in his own world. Manger did not see in their encounter the force of myth but a contact thrust upon two persons
by the impersonal forces of history. For him as for Glatstein, it
is the speech of the body and its difficulties in a precariously
poised world that are worthy of exploration.

At this point it is appropriate to consider the possibility that,
at this moment in his career, David is a tragic hero. This is of
some importance for our understanding of the common matrix
from which these different versions emerge and has as well the
further interest that in general the Jewish Testament eschews
tragedy. The problem of genre here may also be illuminated.
We discover that, for Rilke, David's encounter with Abishag
yields silence instead of speech. Instead of intercourse, in all its
meanings, we have two isolated selves reinforced in their isolation; instead of communication we have—as Rosenzweig puts it
—"the 'selfication' of the hero's self." As hero, "he yearns for
the solitude of demise, because there is no greater solitude than
this." So Rilke's is a poem enacting David's effort to reach out,
even in his old age, beyond his isolating, royal self and, revealing the trajectory of his grand effort, to express in lyric speech
its heroic culmination: silence. If for the moment we follow the
distinctions Rosenzweig works out, it becomes clear that in
Rilke's poem David is indeed a tragic hero at this moment in his
life. "The tragic hero has only one language which completely
corresponds to him," Rosenzweig points out—"precisely keeping silent."[7] Rilke thus charts for us the ways in which David
falls into silence and tragedy, at the end of his life, echoing the
biblical account.

For the sharp-eyed narrator of the Book of Kings, as for Rilke, this situation is ironic. Are there any other moments in the Bible in which David, the sweet singer of Israel, is silenced, his being rendered only by speechlessness? We are reminded of Saul's struggle to express himself, which finds an outlet only in certain mute and tragic actions—the moment, for example, when he tears Samuel's cloak and the prophet draws an appropriate moral from the event: "The Lord has torn the kingdom of Israel from thee this day" (I Samuel 15:28). David's silence, expressed in Rilke's poem, is thus doubly ironic, for was it not in part the fact that David had the gift of speech and song which made it possible for him to supersede Saul?

Rilke's poem meets the biblical narrative at this point in working out a tragic moment. For Rilke this is conclusion; for the biblical narrator it is transition. At the level of genre, the biblical account moves away from tragedy to chart historical patterns—of continuity amid change, for example—which Manger and Glatstein suggest but Rilke chooses not to emphasize. In his, as in the biblical story, we have a tragic node. "In narrative poetry, keeping silent is the rule; dramatic poetry, on the contrary, knows only of speaking, and it is only thereby that silence here becomes eloquent. By keeping silent, the hero breaks down the bridges which connect him with God and the world, and elevates himself out of the fields of personality, delimiting itself and individualizing itself from others in speech, into the icy solitude of self . . . The heroic is speechless."[8]

Where Rilke thus echoes the biblical story, the other writers evade the tragic moment, in its classical guise. Instead of silence, we have Abishag's speech that, in Schmitt's novel, defines David's self as well as her own. This is also true of Glatstein's great poem and to a somewhat lesser extent holds for Manger's cycle. These writers find dialogue central in this story and thereby articulate—instead of Rilke's "drag of the ground" —the heroism possible in the modern world. Theirs is not a Greek heroism of the closed self but a modern sense of self-interpenetrating world and word in mutual self-articulation, in Wordsworthian interfusion. In Rosenzweig's terms, "the hero of the newer tragedy is no longer a 'hero' at all in the old sense, he no longer 'approaches' the spectator 'rigid as antiquity.' He is tossed with a will, wholly receptive, into the to and fro of the world, wholly alive . . . every inch a human being."⁹ In these interpretations of the ancient story, we have characters in a modern sense, as Abishag emerges from the shadowy quasi-anonymity of the biblical account into a local habitation now attached to what formerly was little more than a name, coming forward to challenge David with the special intensity of modern life for the heroic role. For Manger especially, Abishag is hero-ine even more than King David is hero. Instead of lyric hymn, we have the pathos and intelligence of Coleridgean conversa-tion poems; instead of classical Attic tragedy, we have the his-torical novel.

Schmitt's book shows Abishag and David breaking through the gap central to Rilke's poem to form a loving relationship. For the modern novelist, Abishag brings David to his final moment of consciousness—exactly what Rilke shows to be im-possible. Abishag sings to David not only of his glories but his own songs, which she reveals to him as his most lasting legacy to Israel. "I can sing the songs of David," she responds to his query, "even he who is exalted above all the sweet singers in Israel. Nor did they teach me these songs hastily on the night before I departed, that I might sing them before my lord in order to find favor in his sight. Since the day when I first learned what it was to ease the fullness of my heart by pouring my spirit forth from my lips, I sang the songs of David in the fields of Gilead. I know the songs of David as I know the branch that grows across the window near my bed."¹⁰

Here Abishag expresses one of the deepest, most abiding themes of Jewish tradition by showing how David's psalms have become one with the natural world of Israel, adding a transcendent human value to its beauty. It is as song, as mea-sured breath, that Abishag and David encounter each other. "The vibrant music that was within him rose and swelled. Ah, God, he thought, brushing his lips across her hair, how can I turn my back upon this fair, heavy-headed flower that blooms at the edge of my grave?"¹¹ In their relationship, David's music is transformed into the natural rhythms of their world. Through Abishag, David reaches a final understanding of his own role as God's servant and, in Schmitt's novel, learns from Abishag its full meaning. She sings for him, through and with him, the body's song:

> And while she settled him against the heaped cushions, the vibrant music grew within him. The splash and ripple of the spring, the sound of the wind-stirred leaves, the coming and going of her breath—all these became a part of one broad, endless antiphonal song, rising, swelling, opening out above him, encompassing new voices lifted up from the sands of the desert, from the snow-tipped mountains of Lebanon, from the unknown countries beyond Edom and Moab, from the legendary islands in the western sea. Behold, he thought in wonderment, if my heart had ceased to beat while I lay in the churning darkness, the music would not have lessened. [12]

David's songs—the psalms of the Bible—are here, as Jewish tradition has understood them, the very breath of Israel's life. The songs of its messianic king express the gamut of the feelings of all Israel.

Schmitt's novel is a remarkable achievement—supple, lithe, breathtaking—and not least of all its glories is its portrait of Abishag the Shunamite, a fit companion to those of Manger and Glatstein. Her novel captures the way in which David is the center of the messianic imagination of the Jews. In the encounter with Abishag, she points to the profound meaning in the lines every Jewish child knows: *david melekh yisrael hai vekayom* (David king of Israel yet lives).

5
Community and Modernity: Sholom Aleichem

Like a lens focusing the scattered rays that pass through it, the narrator or, as the case may be, the monologist of Sholom Aleichem's stories controls their direction. He (or she) appears in almost every story as a concerned though sympathetic listener, as a brilliant talker, who tries to grasp the purpose of the tales he is told and the kaleidoscopic events he records, as well as understand them in and through his talk. As the meanings filter through this consciousness and emerge from the flow of speech that is the life blood of these stories, the reader participates in the speaker's effort to make sense of these materials. With this relaxed narrator, quick to the humorous possibilities of the complex, seemingly disordered, and even random acts he engages in his storyteller's role, we participate in the effort to locate in the incongruities and coincidences of Eastern European Jewish life a coherence and value that might consolidate fragments into a meaningful whole and thereby establish them as worthy of literary exploration. Through this narrative act of mediation, a wonderfully poised balancing act, Sholom Aleichem explores a penumbra of meaning that is uniquely his own.

In this world the narrative act is never solitary; we have no lyric dialogue of the self addressing itself in the privacy of the mind. Storytelling is a public event, and as the narrator or monologist identifies himself and explains his role, social function, and personal situation in recounting his story, so too he establishes his audience as a figure in the tale.

Geese is my business . . . but you think it's as easy as all that? The first thing you got to do is this: you start buying geese right after *Sukkoth*, in the autumn. You throw them into a coop and keep them there all winter, until December. You feed them and take good care of them. Comes *Hanuka*, you start killing them, and you turn geese into cash. If you think it's so easy to buy them, feed them, kill them, and turn them into cash, you're wrong. First of all—buying the geese. You have to have something to buy them with! And I don't have any reserve money salted away, you know. So I'm forced to go and take a loan from Reb Alter. You know him, don't you? He enjoys squeezing the blood out of you, drop by drop. That is, he doesn't say no right off the bat. But, with his telling you to come tomorrow, the next day, the day after that, he drives you to the breaking point. Then he gets down to work, dragging the interest out of you, adding on extra days. He's some Reb Alter! It's not for nothing he's got such a pot belly and his wife's got a face I wouldn't wish on my enemies and a pair of jowls you could sharpen knives on. Talk of her pearls! Just recently, she had an engagement party for her daughter. Great God! May you and I have a third of what that party cost her. Then I wouldn't have to bother with geese any more. But you ought to see the fellow she got! May God strike me if I'd take the likes of him for my daughter. First of all, he was as bald as an egg. But, anyway, the whole affair is none of my business. I don't like to talk ill of anyone, God forbid, and I like to stay away from backbiting. I'm getting off the track. I'm sorry, but that's a habit of mine. You know what they say: a woman was made with nine measures of talk.[1]

Often the narrator is both teller and listener, and engages his informants in the subtle catechism of the give and take of social discourse. Consciousness thus emerges from these stories in its social dimension; the mind of the narrator is not a precious vessel, discriminating among delicate ideas and sensations that filter through the screen of manners, but a hearty, inquisitive soul bustling about its business of making sense of a busy, complicated world. "You're sadly mistaken, my dear sir. Not all old maids are unhappy and not all bachelors are egoists. You think because sitting here in this room, cigar in mouth and book in hand, you know it all; you've probed deep into the soul and you've got all the answers. Especially since, with the good Lord's help, you've hit upon the right word—psychology. Tsk, tsk. You're really something! It's nothing to be sneezed at— psy-cho-lo-gy. You know what the word means? Psychology means parsley. It looks pretty, smells nice, and, if you put it into a stew, it's tasty. But go chew parsley raw! Not interested, huh?" The subtleties of this narrative consciousness are social rather than psychological (to use these terms in their narrowly defined meanings) and yet, for all that, cast a special light on the situation of the Jew in the modern world. "Then why tell me about psychology? If you want to know what psychology *really* is, sit yourself down and pay close attention to what I'm going to tell you. Afterward, you can have *your* say about how unhappiness and egoism began. Here am I, an old bachelor—and an old bachelor I'm going to be until my dying day! Why? There you go! You see, you've asked why and you're willing to listen to me. That shows true psychology! But the main thing is not to interrupt me with questions. As you know, I've always been a bit touchy and lately I've become more nervous. Don't worry—I'm not crazy, God forbid. Madness—that's more up your alley. You're married. I don't dare go *meshugge*."[2]

The major actions of Sholom Aleichem's stories do not turn on plot denouement or suddenly discovered benefactors. They are not concerned with wealth, happiness, or despair. Instead, such events figure in the story and yet serve only as its vehicle. The major focus is on how they reveal the function and purpose of linguistic action. "Now for the story. I hate long-winded introductions. Her name was Paye, but she was called 'the young widow.' Why? Here we go with whys! What's so difficult about that? They probably called her 'the young widow' because she was young and she was a widow. And think of it! I was younger than her. How much younger? What difference does it make to you? If I say younger, I mean younger. And there were people with wagging tongues who said that since I was a bachelor and she a young widow . . . you get me? Others even congratulated me and wished me luck. Believe it or not! Even if you don't believe me, it's no skin off my back. I don't have to brag to you!" All these characters, the narrator included, reveal themselves as virtuosos of language. "She and I were a couple like you and I are a couple. We just happened to be good friends, no more and no less. We liked each other. Why do I mention it? You see, I knew her husband. Not only did I know him, but we were friendly. That doesn't mean we were friends. I'm just saying we were friendly. Two different things, you know. You can be friendly with someone without being friends. And you can be close friends without being friendly. Anyway, that's my opinion. I'm not asking you what you think."[3] Classical epics begin in the middle of the heroic action. Sholom Aleichem's stories, then, are the epic of the Yiddish language, for the characters of his stories begin always in the middle of a sentence. In these stories, language and language making is central; this entire world is focused on using words to cope with the harsh realities of Eastern European Jewish life and history.[4]

It is as a linguistic action, in tension with this threatening reality, that Sholom Aleichem's stories stake out their own special realm and catch us in their web. Harsher, more materialist critics might dismiss Sholom Aleichem's themes, characters, and events, and with them his whole literary achievement, as nothing more than stories of and by *luftmenschen*, people literally living in and of and by the air, rather than the more substantial world of bread, flesh, and water these solid thinkers inhabit. Their perceptions are accurate with regard to Sholom Aleichem's literary creation, though perhaps such judgments are only possible for those who are convinced that history will inevitably lead to the annihilation of language as its own realm, bringing us into a grim world where language and things are as one—the fate that the world of Eastern European Jewry, and with it much of the best of western culture, had executed for it by Nazis wielding the newspeak technology of the modern world.

Like the characters he presents, Sholom Aleichem pits language against reality and discovers it is not only opposed to language but that reality only exists in and through words. Thus his characters' and narrators' use of language has a special, even heroic dimension. Not only is it their only weapon against a social order basically concerned with their oppression and ultimate extinction; it is also the only means by which the characters can maintain and articulate their own fragile cultural web. The marvelous humor of Sholom Aleichem's stories emerges from the miscomprehensions implicit in the energy and all-encompassing purposiveness with which his characters use words. They address the linguistic realm as if, properly used, it will enable them to recreate reality. With the figure of Sholom Aleichem, the third-person narrator, the reader recognizes the ironic incongruity in trusting to words, even as supple as Yiddish, to overcome the brutal tsarist world, and responds with laughter. And yet there is some peculiar way in which the speaker's power of language produces an ironic victory even in defeat.

The effort to make sense of the world is for Sholom Aleichem a dialectic process interweaving the mean conditions of inhuman baseness with regard to the fundamental human right to live and eat and breathe in the tsar's Eastern Europe, and the spiritual force of illusory goodness and human dignity as manifested in the fragile web of shtetl culture—that realm which was in his time rendered doubly vulnerable by the onslaught of the Black Hundreds as well as the modernizing tendencies of its Jewish inhabitants. Sholom Aleichem reveals the tension between an oppressive political economy and ideal values in various ways. Presenting both poles of this dialectic, he is careful to show their interpenetration during the course of the encounter. It is not so uneven a confrontation as it seems, for if the Russian emperor has many divisions at his beck and call and the process of modernization wields a plethora of seductive ideas and objects, the shtetl still has language, through which alone the others can attain meaning and human value. If the central figure of these stories recounts his or her own story —of events that are catastrophic or situations that are objectively hopeless—yet the very act of telling one's story implies the ability to withstand the onslaught of an army of troubles. Furthermore, these speakers will not allow catastrophe the right to make an appearance in his own person, so to speak. Here troubles are never described frontally or detailed in the objective realism of Balzac or Zola. They surface instead in the flow of speech, like sly devils trying to seduce these characters into acknowledging them as the only reality. And it is when devilish money troubles or politics or pogroms seem about to win the day that Tevye turns to God to talk things over man to man and thereby gain a renewed inner strength. Not that God answers Tevye or makes him rich. Rather, this particular conversation is always stimulating—leading us to imagine that perhaps all talk might conceivably partake of the same renewing possibilities.

Perhaps I can clarify this point by briefly comparing Sholom Aleichem's world and that of the picaresque novel. Both express the nastiness of a reality poised to overwhelm its literary antagonist; both present the individual who must confront the world or be ground under. But—as Claudio Guillén tells us—the picaresque hero is solitary.[5] He has no weapons except his native wits and his sharp use of words. Still, he accepts the values of the world that time and again robs him. We should be clear that the authors of the original Spanish picaresque works, *conversos* living in Spain's ambivalent sixteenth and seventeenth centuries, were thereby casting the rogue's appetite for experience, his conviction that with luck he too could climb to the top, in an ironic and satiric light. In the picaresque novel, the rogue's desires make him gullible by experience and thereby force him to give it independent life. In effect, he is part of the mosaic of the tense, violent, and complex world he is confronting. As Joseph Silverman has pointed out, he articulates its multiple facets, refusing to deny any of them, and in this way affirms its multiplicity of potentials by practicing *el arte de no renunciar a nada*.[6] Sholom Aleichem's protagonists are cut from a different cloth. Then too they speak Yiddish, while the nasty realities of their world mutter and command in Russian, whereas the rogue and his environment encounter each other in all the varieties and dialects of the king's Castilian. Ultimately, when at the end of that energetic first picaresque novel, *Lazarillo de Tormes*, we laugh at Lazarillo's willingness to deceive himself and accept his cuckoldry in return for safety and relative ease, we also distance ourselves from the brutal world that has tormented as well as seduced him into its values and institutionalized deceptions.

Confronted by Sholom Aleichem's characters who, unable to change fundamental conditions, pour out their life in words to us, we encounter figures toward whom we have an ironic yet loving relation. If pícaro and schlemiel both confess to us, the reader, the pride of the former in managing to triumph over a brutal world in its own terms is always manifest and ultimately punishable; the latter is clearly separate from his violent antagonistic environment and does not internalize its values. The pícaro ultimately hopes to pass for an hidalgo; the Jew hopes rather to continue to be himself. The Spanish rogue of Jewish ancestry has visions of upward social mobility, the Eastern European schlemiel hopes to survive just because of his failure to manipulate disaster into personal success. In refusing to internalize its irrational, impersonal, hostile and aggressive values, Sholom Aleichem's heroes do not confuse their own ethos with their surroundings. Danger is external to them; life goes on for them in terms of their own values. Unlike Kafka's heroes who internalize the outside order, Sholom Aleichem's protagonists cannot conceive of participating in the horror confronting them, for they are secure in their universe of meaning. As Ruth Wisse notes, "Sholom Aleichem's schlemiel, for all his simplicity, or näiveté, or weakness, or dreaminess, or predisposition for misfortune, or whatever tendency it is that makes him a schlemiel, retains a very firm sense of his distinct self. His sense of personal identity and worth is not seriously disrupted by the bombardment of environmental harrassments. The schlemiel represents the triumph of identity despite the failure of circumstance."[7] Given the conditions of his world, the schlemiel can hope only to hang on. Toward this modest and humble desire, we have in Sholom Aleichem's world an understanding relation of laughter.

Conceiving of writing as a solace, Sholom Aleichem devised a method for defending the self against a reality so unpleasant as to offer no possibility of hope for amelioration. In his work the Jews are a schlemiel people—and yet are able to turn defeat into victory through the power of laughter. The trick is "to convert disaster into a verbal triumph," through the application of an almost Talmudic ingenuity of interpretation. Avoidance, sublimation, theoretical reversal all helped them use an inappropriate response to transform a "desperate moment into a pleasurable one."[8] Freud's mapping of this technique reveals its psychological mechanism; it had as well a crucial social dimension.

Folk humor found its Yiddish voice in challenging "not the political status quo or the prestige of the Biblical canon," but the emphasis on learning in Jewish culture and its implicit claims for the power of the scholar and the sacred Hebraic tradition. Generating a host of fools, Yiddish culture satirized the pretensions of learning, notably in its Chelm stories. Here, when a problem must be solved, the Chelmites come up with a formula theoretically correct but practically absurd. To capture the moon, they throw a burlap bag over the top of a barrel filled with water. Subsequently, they are incredulous when they hear reports of the moon's appearance elsewhere. Trying to push a mountain further away from their town, these people reveal their capacity for belief. Thieves steal the jackets they have dropped behind them. They conclude that they have pushed far enough, since the jackets are no longer visible. These Chelm jokes ridicule thought, dissociated from practical experience, just as the hasidic movement protested against the arid intellectualism of Talmudic scholasticism. "All the strains of a highly intellectualistic culture are relaxed in these tales of incredible foolishness and innocence."[9] The high culture believed it might find a way out of the intolerable situation of the Jews, through a better understanding of their tradition perhaps or a clear articulation of methods to bring the messianic days closer, whether of Sabbetai Zevi or of Theodore Herzl. Against its pride in the process of intellect as action, the jokes of the folk culture like the work of Sholom Aleichem stand as ironically clear-sighted recognitions of the reality of the Jews' lot in a world where the tsar is succeeded by Stalin, and brutal Nazis by equally crazed fedayeen and murdering "liberationists."

In Sholom Aleichem's world, to be foolish is not to be dumb, for it is these simple folk who speak wittily and in sophisticated self-deprecatory modes. For them, speaking to that ever-present audience always hovering on the edges of the tale, and occasionally even entering into it to scold or comfort, is to engage in the difficult dialectic not of action but the more complex practice of self-definition. Since their values are in conflict with those of their non-Jewish environment, these speakers constantly juggle two worlds—and yet are marvelously poised as they display pyrotechnic brilliance in words. For it is in language alone that this conflict and this complex questioning of the nature of meaning and value can be expressed. In this world, everything becomes words—or the pauses and gestures that punctuate their flow.

Consider the speaker of *Geese*, a woman who elaborates the art of raising geese for us, not because she is successful at it but because it is all she knows how to do to survive. The pressure of her talk is surely that of someone just hanging on to sanity in intolerable conditions, as she finds a way to raise her birds in the corner of an urban hovel shared with two families in a condition of extreme stress. Somehow her rambling conversation and self-deprecating refrain become the embodiment of her marginal situation. "What a town! You'd think someone would care. Poor people were dying of cold, they were swelling up with hunger. The children were falling like flies. But it wasn't so terrible, because only the poor were dying. May God not punish me. I'm not talking ill of anyone. I don't want to gossip. But, I seem to have lost the thread of the story. Sorry—but that's a bad habit of mine. You know what they say: a woman was made with nine measures of talk." As the story unfolds, her tale encompasses a widening circle. While judging herself she manages to loose an array of satiric volleys at her own folk. "Goose-meat. You'd be in some pickle if you only depended on the goose-meat . . . There's one woman I know who buys up every single neck I have. Even if there's four dozen, she takes them all. It's her husband, she says. He goes wild for necks and white meat . . . Well, what do you say to that? Like the saying goes: the dead look the way they eat! And you ought to see that woman's husband! Compared to my husband, he looks like a man of thirty, God bless him, although he's a good ten years older than my Nakhman-Ber."[10]

Once she has our attention, all her complaints can be paraded. Not that they can be remedied, but it does the heart good to unburden itself. "Although my husband doesn't do a stitch of work besides poring over his books, when he comes home, he doesn't grunt like other men and say: 'Listen here, bring some food!' The first thing he does when he comes home from the study room in the synagogue, is pick up a book. He reads it and sighs quietly." A strict code governs self-expression. Its rules make it possible for language to serve as a marker bracketing off an unpleasant reality while acknowledging for the moment its existence.

That means he's hungry. But he'll never say it out loud. What, then? He groans, puts his hand to his heart, and says, "Oh, me." That shows he's really starving! "Want something to eat?" I ask him. "All right," he says. No matter how much I tell him, "I don't understand you. You got a mouth, why don't you use it? Why do you have to sit there and moan?"—it does no good. Go speak to the wall. I'd like to see what would happen if, on purpose, I didn't feed him for three days. But do you think he's got *that* many bees in his bonnet? How can a scholar like him be such a ninny? If with what he knows, he'd just be a little more of a pusher, don't you think he could be the village rabbi?

For a moment, we think, words will lead to action. Instead they enable us to confront the grim premises of this world without giving in to them. "But, then, what would we do with our old rabbi? Come to think of it—what are we going to do with our old cantor? We just got a new one, you know. We needed him like a hole in the head. We got him so that the old cantor could starve because—after all—he wasn't much of a pauper before-hand, anyway. Why'd all this come about? Because the village rich man likes good singing. You want to hear good voices? Go to the theater and they'll sing you to death there."[11]

If there is room for emotion, there is no possibility of making that an engine of change. These words become lightning rods that draw off the tension and allow life such as it is to continue. "If I were only a man I'd show them a thing or two. Boy, would I take care of them! Do you think I have any squabbles with them? Nah. I just hate their guts. I can't stand those rich big-shots. Spiders and rich men! May God not punish me. I'm not belittling a soul, and I don't like to criticize anyone behind his back. But I'm getting off the track. Well, that's the way I am, you'll have to excuse me. You know what they say: a woman has nine measures of talk in her." And then the startling thing happens. As she talks, her trade becomes an allegory of her own life and that of the daughters she is trying so desperately to raise. Like the geese who must be cared for constantly, fed and cleaned in order to be sold and killed for a measly profit, so too the girls of this world are fattened for the slaughter. "Well, what you get out of the geese . . . Don't think that you're in clover once you've sold the goose-fat, all the meat, and the giblets. If geese didn't have feathers and down, the whole business wouldn't be worth its weight in salt. When I start, that is before I even put them into their coops, I feel them under the armpits, and scrape away the little bit of down I find there. There's even more after they're killed. Then I take the feathers and the down separately, and prepare work for the whole winter. The nights are plenty long and there's time enough for plucking. So I sit and pluck. I have a little help, too. My girls."[12]

The speaker hovers on the verge of comprehending the full meaning of her own life through her talk—sad, to be sure, yet still radiant with value like her struggle to support herself by raising geese.

> Girls aren't boys, you know. Boys go to school. But what do girls do? Girls are like a bunch of geese; they sit at home, eat, and wait to grow up. I sit them down in front of a sieve and tell them to start plucking feathers. "If you do," I say, "tomorrow, God willing, I'll smear some goose-fat on a piece of bread and give it to you. Better yet, I'll make a soup out of gizzards." You should see them rush to work. It's nothing to sneeze at—a soup made out of gizzards. What can I do? We don't even see a piece of meat all week long, not counting the Sabbath. If I didn't sell geese, I don't know what I'd do with my children all week long.

This ironic realization does not come at the expense of the speaker but in and through her language. "Like this, they manage to get hold of a little gullet, a gizzard, a head, a foot, a drop of goose-fat. The smell alone is enough for them. When I lived in Yente's house—and I don't wish this on anyone—my neighbor Genesi told me: 'You know, when *Hanuka* rolls around and you start messing around with your Passover geese and kosher-for-Passover goose-fat, a new life comes into my little gang. The smell of the cooking alone makes them dizzy and they think that they're eating goose-meat.' "[13] This is, in fact, a realization *of* her language, in some magical way uncovered simply because she talks with and to us.

Her language is not a vehicle opposed to her true self but the fullness of her very being. It is only in talking that she truly lives and thus can discover who she is. Even if her discovery is a sad and uncomfortable truth about her situation, it is nevertheless transcended by language, by her flow of talk, despite the harsh rabbinic judgment she never stops applying to herself.

Sholom Aleichem thereby expressed what the Jews "instinctively felt was the right and true judgment of their experience: a judgment of love through the medium of irony." He is, in Irving Howe's phrase, "the great poet of Jewish humanism and Jewish transcendence over the pomp of the world." In his writing, the Jews found consolation. If he celebrated their tradition and defended their style of life and their urge to dignity, he was as well their judge. His language functioned as an oral performance that validated—perhaps because it was written down—the staying power of the culture of Eastern European Jewry. His "Yiddish is one of the most extraordinary verbal achievements of modern literature, as important in its way as T. S. Eliot's revolution in the language of English verse or Berthold Brecht's infusion of street language into the German lyric. Sholom Aleichem uses a sparse and highly controlled vocabulary; his medium is so drenched with irony that the material which comes through it is often twisted and elevated into direct tragic statement—irony multiplies upon itself to become a deep winding sadness. Many of his stories are monologues, still close to the oral folk tradition, full of verbal by-play, slow in pace, winding in direction, but always immediate and warm in tone." In Sholom Aleichem "everything that is deepest in the ethos of the east European Jews is brought to fulfillment and climax. He is, I think, the only modern writer who may truly be said to be a culture-hero, a writer whose work releases those assumptions of his people, those tacit gestures of bias, which undercut opinion and

go deeper into communal life than values."[14] His verbal construct provides understanding for his people because they find
their voice in it.

The language is rich; that compensates for the poverty it
speaks of. The words seem endless: perhaps that makes up for
the narrow possibilities they must cope with. The names are
multiple, because their overdetermination is needed to baffle
the simple facts of misery. Exuberant self-indulgence of the "description of disaster takes the sting out of . . . failure." Thus by
the very richness of his account, the speaker transforms "failure
into a declamatory success. If we measure life, and language, by
intensities of experience rather than by objective tests of achievement, the schlemiel is no loser." This satire "mocks the life-style
that substitutes verbal riches for tangible comfort," and the
"descriptions of bloodspitting, sickly children, social ostracism,
and vicious poverty, emphasize the full price each family paid
for a schlemiel as breadwinner." Nevertheless, as Ruth Wisse
makes clear, "Sholom Aleichem is making poverty the metaphor for spiritual wealth, and using the superabundance of language, particularly the rich veins of wit and humor, to suggest
the cultural affluence that may be nourished by physical depri-
vation. The schlemiel is the bearer of this ironic meaning."[15]

Language occasionally serves as the plot of a story. Consider
"Happy New Year," a compact account of the most feared event
in peaceful times in Eastern European Jewish history: the advent
of an incorruptible royal official who sees his purpose in life to
consist in enforcing the antisemitic laws of the Russian empire.
Against such Christian purity the Jews have no recourse, for he
banishes the entire system of bribes which made it possible for
them to continue to exist in a world that gave them no room to
breathe. "Happy New Year" is told by a narrator who addresses
his audience as "brother Jews" and, placing his story in the pro-
tective coloration of a biblical tale by making Tsar Nicholas
into Ahasuerus and the incorruptible village official into
Haman, by sprinkling his tale with Hebrew, he keeps the Russian peasants from understanding it. It is an account of how the
narrator's grandfather outwitted the government and, like a
modern Mordechai (with the aid of his rabbi's advice and some
marvelous horses), saved his people from destruction. There is

a double plotline—how the narrator's grandfather got his role from the rabbi, learning some powerful phrases to use for the occasion, and how the actual outwitting of Russian officialdom is accomplished.

Briefly, the horses—twin full-blooded spotless roans—are purchased, no matter the exorbitant price, from a gypsy at the fair on the rabbi's advice and paraded around the tsar's palace. When a royal official asks him the price of the horses, grandfather answers, "I'm not a horse-dealer." Since he can't buy or steal the horses, the official will expropriate them. "You know," he says, "the Czar liked your horses," in a phrase filled with the ambiguous implications the powerful love to use in addressing their inferiors. Grandfather responds spontaneously, perhaps as the narrator says because "if it's fated, God gives you bright ideas." After all the rabbi must have had his reasons for outlining this course of action to him. If the tsar likes the horses, grandfather says, "then my horses can be his horses," by this simple and seemingly unambiguous statement undercutting the unpleasant possibilities present in the official's sentence. Grandfather is duly ushered into the tsar's presence and continues this strange uncommercial bargaining process in the courtyard, though he is petrified at the sight of—as he calls him—Mr. Big.

These horses have, of course, "some sort of mystic power," and the tsar himself "couldn't get enough of them," staring at them "for an hour, showing them off to the court," in short "falling in love with them at first sight" (a witty reference to the biblical description of Ahasuerus' response to Esther). When the tsar asks grandfather's price, he repeats, "I don't sell horses. But if his majesty has taken a liking to the horses, and if his majesty will not be angry with me, let the horses be led into his majesty's stables. That's where they belong." The tsar wants to make sure the horses are not a bribe and after a good bit of discussion considers accepting them. After all, grandfather assures him: "Your majesty. King! I swear that I have no underhanded intentions, and I'm not the sort who likes to bluff or trick anyone. I don't ask a thing of his majesty. But I would consider it an honor and the greatest of favors if I could be worthy of having my horses in his majesty's stables and if his majesty would ride them."[16] Grandfather thereupon leaves the courtyard, is invited into the palace, smokes a cigar with the tsar, has tea with him—served of course by the tsarina—and tells about the incorruptible village official.

It is important to understand how the linguistic energy of the story manifests itself—in its use of biblical nicknames for Russian rulers, for one thing, and in the interweaving of the rabbi's advice and the actual encounter with the tsar for another, as well as in terming the tsar "Mr. Big" and the official "Buttons." Both these titles express the social roles the men play from the standpoint of the Jews. Through grandfather's circumlocutions, we encounter the realities of Jewish life under the tsar. They form the conditions of that life. Rather than objecting to its injustice, Reb Anshel takes them as givens—the only material he has to work with. By his analogy to their biblical traditions, he identifies the Jews as a self-deprecating group who by their nature give bribes. The real situation is humorously twisted by this conceptualization, and it is from the disparity between reality and speech that our laughter emerges.

Furthermore, the rabbi's later exegetical discussion provides similar comedy. " 'In the chapter of admonition in Leviticus,' the *rebbe* began with closed eyes, as was the custom, 'there is a curse, the simple meaning of which we cannot understand. The Bible says that God will send you a nation whose language you will not be able to understand. The question then arises, what sort of a curse is that? Let me repeat it—God will send you someone whose language you won't understand.' " Without words, the Jews will be helpless—they will no longer be themselves.

> How is that possible? That the gentiles (forgive the proximity) don't understand our language—well, that's natural —that's why they're gentiles. But that a Jew won't understand what the gentile is talking about? Where's the connection? Is there anything a Jew doesn't understand? If so, we have to interpret the verse differently. God will send forth a nation whose language you will not understand really means that God will send a gentile whom you won't be able to *talk* to. In other words, he'll be as clean as a whistle. His palms won't be greasable. And a gentile who doesn't take bribes is a catastrophe.[17]

As a result of this interpretive sally, the Jews begin to discover the true dimensions of their sad lot. Nevertheless, the ensuing laughter and pleasure at transforming an intolerable situation into a pseudo-biblical prophecy enables them to cope with it out of a pride of language that by its action makes room for them to exist in a miserable reality. Persuaded of the Jews need to give by the wonder-working horses, the tsar replaces Buttons with a corruptible official just in time for the Jews to celebrate a happy new year.

The narrator quotes an occasional Hebrew word to keep nearby gentiles from understanding him. In this way, Sholom Aleichem alludes to the mystical traditions with which Jews have surrounded their holy tongue and the sacred text on which the story is self-consciously modeled. Thereby his tale expresses the structure and context of Yiddish, written in Hebrew characters and a German syntax, supplemented by a Hebrew grammar, with a vocabulary drawn from the linguistic groups with which the Jews of the West have had contact. The story also enacts the latent theme of shtetl culture, which is founded in and on a sacred Hebrew text, whose relevant meanings are unpacked in Yiddish. Like that culture, its purposive action focuses on the use of language to seduce, negotiate, bargain, protect, save, redeem, and by means of all these to ensure the survival of the Jews for another year.

Language is at the center of Sholom Aleichem's world. It is possible to multiply examples: in "On Account of a Hat," the main character's confusion leads him to believe he has changed his identity by putting on a Russian officer's cap, and yet this tale of his foolishness allows us to triumph over it. Similarly, the impeccable reasoning of the narrator of "Three Calendars" leads him to wrong inferences, because it is grounded in the paranoia of the persecuted Jew. Instead of selling Jewish calendars and Jewish newspapers, he ends up selling "French" postcards, using pornography as a disguise for his role as a disseminator of Jewish materials—of language, by means of which Jews can locate their experience and celebrate their holidays.

All these stories predicate social experience not by status, riches, or natural experience, but in terms of the logic and purposes of language. Even marriage becomes a matter for words— for negotiations, bargains, and even scandals. They are rich feasts of words, and yet resemble a dinner without a main course. There is little concern for geography; history is almost completely absent, except in the mythical modeling on traditional texts; and the body's world, so important to twentieth-century writers, is transformed into mere linguistic action.

These are peculiarly appropriate defects, for their very absence articulates the real lack of these experiences in the world of Eastern European Jewry. Now it is not my purpose to argue that the shtetl produced no heirs and that its inhabitants were barren. I want to point to the ways in which Sholom Aleichem's world mirrors the shtetl and allows only language, the vehicle for social experience, entry into its realm. This language expresses the life processes of the shtetl, which turned everything into the means for its survival and could not recognize the value of nature for itself, so that its young had to rebel and leave it, as did Bialik and Babel.

Sholom Aleichem's world is remarkably intense, vivid, and narrow. It is without a politics of Zionist transformation that might put its airy force in touch with the realities of land, nationhood, violence, and modern technology. Even the politics of its inhabitants rely on scandal mongering—an activity that depends on the active deployment of words rather than institutional structures for its force. Sholom Aleichem's world articulates a vision close to that of the great Jewish historian, Simon Dubnow, who believed that language alone would ensure the cultural autonomy of the Jewish people. It was the secret guarantee of Jewish national existence throughout the arduous centuries of its exile, its portable culture enacted in Yiddish. So long as the Jews had room to take care of their own cultural affairs, organize their community, and speak their own tongue, Odessa was as good as Tel Aviv. Dubnow, it is important to point out, stuck to his beliefs even when the Germans entered his village and led him off to the mass grave he shares with the millions of his fellow Yiddish speakers. In short, Sholom Aleichem's stories embody the ways in which language determines everything in the shtetl.

As historian Jacob Katz has pointed out, it was opinion that defined this world—its power, purposes, and values. "Concentration of the various sources of power in the same hands gives one the impression that this society maintained a well-defined social classification in its structure at all times. The place of each person in the social concentration manifested itself not in distinguishable lines of demarcation setting class apart from class, but in the verdict of public opinion, which set a value on the position of each individual."[18] Public opinion, as detailed of course in gossip, was the dominant and supporting institution of this culture. It lived quite actually in its talk. Katz's analysis helps to illuminate the gossipy pleasure of so much of Sholom Aleichem's work, for despite the rabbinical injunction, it was gossip that determined social value, sustaining and shaping the web of culture by enacting the buzz and hum of Jewish experience in the world of the shtetl. It served as the secular counterpart to the chanting and Talmudic gyrations of the intellectuals in their House of Study.

Having noted the important elements absent in Sholom Aleichem's work, it is crucial also to see how he turns these defects into part of the triumph of his art. Here we must look at an important story, "Three Widows," in which a bachelor tells of his relations with three generations of women, each of whom he loves and almost proposes to, and whose collective tragedy he recounts. In this account, we have a parablelike recapitulation of Jewish history in Eastern Europe.

The narrator of "Three Widows," a confirmed old bachelor, describes three generations of shtetl life, through the lives of three widows and the deaths of their husbands. The first, Pini, was a good friend of the bachelor's, in many ways resembling him. Pini was clever, self-educated, rich, but down to earth—he didn't aim for the moon. Pini died as he had lived, without much fuss. He came home sick one day; six days later he was dead. The disagreement between the doctors didn't help him any. "One said operate, the other said don't. Meanwhile the patient died."[19] All very ordinary. But Pini's death makes life chaotic for his widow Paye and our narrator. He couldn't make the simple statement that would restore order to his and Paye's life by asking her to marry him. After all, he was only a friend not a blood relative, and the requirement of Levirate marriage did not fall upon him. Instead he remains only a friend of the family, aiding in the daughter Rose's upbringing, paving the way for the second tragedy.

The second husband, Shapiro, was manager, boss, and

supervisor of a distillery. A good honest businessman, dragged into scandal by his employers, he is left to take responsibility for their crimes when they run away to America with the money Shapiro had earned for them. He is charged with fraudulent bankruptcy and takes poison to avoid humiliation. The narrator is again incapable of declaring his love for Rose, the second widow. The same pattern of life is maintained, our bachelor taking an active role in bringing up the daughter Feygele, but unable to restore real order by marrying either Rose or Paye.

Along comes a third generation of suitors. The cultured bourgeoisie of the second generation are replaced by the disrespectful Marxist revolutionaries of the third. Feygele marries Gruzevitsh, the student of chemistry. Three days later he "was taken to jail over a small matter. They just happened to run across a whole storehouse of bombs and dynamite. And since he was a chemist and a famous one at that suspicion fell on him."[20] Chaos again ensues, to be replaced by grief once the hanging is over.

The narrator has come to the end of his story. Three generations have attempted to live in the world in three different ways, reflecting the shtetl's changing relationship to the outside world. Three husbands die, all victims of outside powers—of quarreling doctors who can't make up their minds how to treat their patient, of business fraud and a frameup, and the intolerable repression of the tsar that foments violent revolution. The walls of the shtetl are being pierced by violent, even new forces, and no one seems prepared or able to control them.

The attempts of the three women are even more pathetic than those of their husbands. All three are exactly the same; the pattern of their lives is identical. It is simple for the bachelor to fall in love with each of them. Nothing at all has changed in the shtetl, nothing has even begun, the narrator tells us: "We lived in memories, in the past. Three widows—three lives. Not complete lives, but half lives. Not half lives either—but fragments. Just the start of lives. Each had started so well, so poetically. It flashed for a moment then was snuffed out." The narrator adds, "I'm not talking about myself, I don't count."[21] The irony is that the whole story is about the narrator and why he doesn't count, focusing on the role of storyteller and revealing how there is no more place in the world for him than for any of the characters he creates.

Interwoven in the stories of the three widows and their husbands is the bachelor's story of his attempt to make sense of the world. Life is passing him by. He is completely impotent, carrying around a fantasy life in his mind, which he has no hope to put into action. Three widows and he can't keep the spark of life burning in any of them, or in himself. He lacks the force of speech that defines the world and, framing it, enables us to act in it, the power to put the world in order with the proper words.

He is certainly no Talmudist of the secular life, for he cannot utter "Just the one word and we could have been man and wife."[22] Nor is he simply a secular writer or a cabalist—an ironic and tragic weakness in one who fancies himself a storyteller. He lacks the power to deal with the force penetrating the shtetl. So he's not much of a socialist either and can't save Gruzevitsh from hanging. He cannot speak of love and scorns those novelists whose descriptions of nature "resemble nature as much as I do the Turkish sultan." He cannot even be a Zionist. He can no more live with nature than he can with history. His greatest fear is of being simply pushed out of the picture, of discovering that, to the young, "We're nobodies. We don't exist."[23] The bachelor and his widows lack concrete identity in the world. He can only retaliate with artful talk. Theories change, the world changes, but art may last forever. As does his interminable talk.

There is no art in the usual sense in the narrator's world. There are no fixed points of reference, no defined characters to create a complete story. We have only the fragments of lives, poetically begun. Inspiration is repeatedly snuffed out before it becomes reality. The narrator can only lament, "Why have I thrown my life away so foolishly . . . Each one of them might have been mine and still might be."[24] He never leaves his inner fantasy world. He can only return to his diary until it is time to play cards and be witty again.

Sholom Aleichem ironically makes a great story out of these

tragi-comic failures, and art of a special kind from his narrator's artlessness. "Three Widows" is finally the story of its bachelor narrator and his consciousness of impotence in the face of the overwhelming power of the real world. He cannot succeed in it because as a Jew he has no effective political and social structures that can bring the violent world to heel. Its force appears as the interruptions that punctuate and even threaten the flow of his narrative. But from these interruptions the bachelor makes a narrative that gives shape to the intrusions of a violent world, by defining his own identity.

In a very special way, he is the genius of Yiddish, able to encounter the worst, sympathetic to all, subtle, keen-minded yet not harsh, and alas without the powerful intrusive force of the prophetic tongue—of Hebrew—which can reshape reality with a word. His is a language that can respond even to the worst events by making an ironic gesture, a shrug of the shoulders, and life such as it is can continue. It is a language of loving attention, like the bachelor's attitude to the three widows who yet manage to ensure the continued existence of the Jews by giving birth to a new generation. This is a language and an art that redeems a bitter world of fragments—"just the start of lives" never allowed to be concluded—by its secular power to make a story of them.

That is the marginal world he can make—a story world. It is a world built out of nothing more than social talk in a secular tongue. As language, as talk in its most sophisticated sociological form—as opinion and gossip—this art form redeems. As such it has its special place in constituting the world through the language by means of which all of us each day and every waking moment are made human. Here Sholom Aleichem's world echoes the response of Pérez de Ayala, who at the climax of his novel *Belarmino and Apolonio* has his self-taught philosopher of language remark on the necessary links between words, speech, and life. " 'That sweet and delicious tongue of yesteryear has become untied. Speak, speak, my dear, beloved friend.' But Belarmino, teary-eyed, holds out his arm and says in a dark voice, 'Not now; not now. We will speak some other day; we will speak, my very dear Colignon; we will speak until our hearts melt and become pure saliva, and the saliva, words, and the words like the wind.'"[25] Belarmino's comment articulates the real force of mere words. According to Jewish tradition, it is this process of language making that links our world to God's, whose spirit—the Hebrew word is *ruach*, which also means wind—hovers over the world.

6
Folk Speech and Holy Tongue: Agnon and Borges

On first reading, the language of S. Y. Agnon's stories is transparent. Dreamlike, mystical, detailing the hidden movements of spirit revealed and explored in momentary glimpses—an image in a mirror, the search for a meal after a day without food, desire springing up between man and woman on the day they are divorced—Agnon's Hebrew seems a clear medium leaving hardly a trace behind. And yet, upon subsequent readings, it becomes clear that his words are part of the wonder of his work. They grow organically out of classical Jewish tradition, echo in their syntax the dialectic sentences of the Mishnah and Talmud, as well as some Yiddish rhythms, and are suffused in an erotic flush appropriate to writing that often issues into midrashic commentary on love in the modern world. His language demands to be attended to, like a dream calling attention to itself or a narrator telling a story about his friends that turns out to be a tale detailing the structure of his own psyche.

This aspect of Agnon's work links him not to Kafka, to whom he has been often compared, but to Borges, in whose work we find a similar interest in language as self-conscious dreaming. Both writers seek to evoke the dreamlike moment in which the symbol-making activity of language is half hidden yet half revealed, just as spiritual and psychic events are linked to the language-making act. They also share a common effort to revitalize their respective languages by connecting them not merely to the argot of the street—a concern of many Argentinian and Israeli writers of this century—but to a classical tradition available to Agnon in Jewish sources and to Borges in certain favorite writers whom he claims with good reason form a dominant tradition in western culture. Here is Agnon:

> Raphael sat and wrote. He wrote his Torah scroll day and night, interrupting the work only for prayers with the congregation and for the recitation of the kaddish. A prayer shawl was spread over the clean table, its fringes drooping below the table and getting intertwined with the fringes of the little prayer shawl he wore. On the prayer shawl lay a lined sheet of parchment dazzling in its whiteness as the sky itself in its purity.
>
> From morning to evening the quill wrote on the parchment and beautiful black letters glistened and alighted on the parchment as birds upon the snow on the Sabbath when the Song of Moses is read. When he came to the writing of the great and awesome Name he would go down to the ritual bath and immerse himself.
>
> Thus he sat and wrote until he completed the entire Torah scroll.[1]

And here is Borges:

> Abulgualid Muhammad Ibn-Ahmad ibn-Muhammad ibn-Rushd (a century this long name would take to become Averroes, first becoming Benraist and Avenryz and even Aben-Rassad and Filius Rosadis) was writing the eleventh chapter of his work *Tahafut-ul-Tahafut* (Destruction of Destruction), in which it is maintained, contrary to the Persian ascetic Ghazali, author of the *Tahafut-ul-falasifa* (Destruction of Philosophers), that the divinity knows only the general laws of the universe, those pertaining to the species, not to the individual. He wrote with slow sureness, from right to left; the effort of forming syllogisms and linking vast paragraphs did not keep him from feeling like a state of wellbeing, the cool and deep house surrounding him. In the depths of the siesta amorous doves called huskily; from some unseen patio arose the murmur of a fountain; something in Averroes, whose ancestors

came from the Arabian deserts, was thankful for the constancy of the water. Down below were the gardens, the orchard; down below, the busy Guadalquivir and then the beloved city of Cordova, no less eminent than Bagdad or Cairo, like a complex and delicate instrument, and all around (this Averroes felt also) stretched out to the limits of the earth the Spanish land, where there are few things, but where each seems to exist in a substantive and eternal way.[2]

In both stories we encounter scholars whose life is their writing and which in both instances becomes a complicated and highly charged action. They take an erotic pleasure in it, only to discover the irony of seeking fulfillment in writing luminous mystic symbols. Borges and Agnon share a common strategy, bypassing realistic expectations and creating a dreamlike world, which moves the reader and the action of the tale into a suspended realm where words and deeds take on all meanings at the same time.

Both scholars create a world in which words have ceremonial and ritualistic functions. For them, they articulate fateful questions and thus serve as thematic centers for many of their stories. Raphael and Averroes enact traditional word rituals that catch them in the meaning they seek to elicit; their words become their fate in an ironic and oblique act of meaning making that ultimately is reflexive rather than referential. Thus their work becomes a structural principle of the texts in which they figure. Symbolic inhabitants, they project the symbol-making activity of their worlds as its crucial act.

As they write, Raphael and Averroes experience a generalized sensation of sexual well-being. For Agnon, word making is linked through eros to that divine love which bestowed its sacred text and language upon Israel; for Borges, language is the divine guarantee of humanity. Raphael and Averroes nest in their words. Writers, they are written up. This is the central tension of the stories: the self is defined by the very activity that is predicated of it. This tension of doubling leads to an infinite regression, until we are perplexed as to what is and is not the writer's self, where it begins and language ends. Just as the scholar or writer of these stories is symbolized in his own symbol-making activities, so too the detective of other stories is entangled in his own web. Words become the vessels of eros. In the worlds of both writers this erotic potential of language issues into dream actions; their stories tremble on the edge of a revelation about the origins and nature of language.

As word and world makers, Agnon and Borges have carefully wrought elusive literary personae. The secret of their worlds encompasses their own role as writers. Availing himself of Talmudic and Aggadic traditions, Agnon constructs a persona in which the writer is the embodiment of the enigmatic puzzle of the tale: he is its riddle and meaning. Wily and almost elvish, Agnon seems to have delighted in playing such a role in his daily life—especially for the benefit of earnest critics. Borges has similarly set a secret of his own past as part of the myth of his work, leaving clues that the solution is in the recognition that he is Jewish. In his autobiographical comment, Borges tells us his grand-uncle was an Italian-Jewish engineer who brought the first horse-drawn tramcars to Argentina. His wife's sister, Fanny Haslam, came from England to live with them. She subsequently married Borges' grandfather and bequeathed the writer an English heritage.[3] Jewish origins are thus at best tangential for Borges. Yet he has found the Cabala fascinating and, as in Agnon, its themes and symbols have a prominent place in his work. Perhaps the secret Borges is constantly skirting is the recognition that like Agnon he has made the world a text in which his own life is to be read.

Their shared concern with dreams as literary theme and narrative structure is also a way of signaling the two writers' lack of interest in the realist's business of making and matching.[4] Neither is concerned with world making on the realistic model; the fiction of both tends to be short, precise, and probing, even inquisitorial as Borges puts it. Their work lacks the voluminous energy of Balzac or Dickens; it has instead the rapier edge of a Pascalian pensee. Borges and Agnon articulate the continuing process of writing in their work, eliciting the various potentials implicit in this act. Thus a typical character in one of Borges' stories searches for a killer and finds himself in the form of his enemy; one of Agnon's protagonists seeks a place for the night and finds the alphabet in which his name is written. Both characters, lacking the identifying mark of a personal name—the signature of the realistic novel—yet partake of the mythic naming power latent everywhere in their language, which emerges as they try to discover the nature of their identities by probing into those of their worlds and words.

Intellectuals embarking on a linguistic adventure—which turns out to be a search for the ultimate secrets of language and naming—figure prominently in the work of both writers. The initial quest becomes central; writer, reader, world, and word are implicated. The tales enact the entanglement of consciousness and language, often concluding in an event that makes character and reader aware of the meanings implicit in this process. The writing activity, a figure in the story as well as its constitutive action, becomes both image and mirror. Closer to lyric than to realistic story, these tales do not allow us the experience of completeness and resolution so crucial to the realistic novel. They lead to other stories and other writers, to imagined, not yet realized worlds, thereby allowing us a glimpse of the unending process of word and language making that is central to the continuing action and process of consciousness envisioned by Borges and Agnon.

Two of Agnon's novellas are particularly relevant to this theme. *Betrothed* and *Edo and Enam*, written within a few years of each other and published together in the collected works as *Ad Hena* (roughly translatable as To This Point or Thus Far),[5] are about scholars who collect, analyze, examine—and receive great joy and spiritual reward from their work. Both men bring unknown worlds to light and life; both are in love with sleep walkers. Awakening them with magical code words they have just deciphered, the scholars gain access to the hidden worlds of which these women are the muses. *Edo and Enam* ends in a love-death that results from the protagonist's effort to decode the hidden language that connects its characters. In *Betrothed*, the heroine Shoshana awakens from her sleep to run a race with her friends (nicknamed "the planets" and associated with various aspects of the Zodiac), who are also her rivals for the scholar's love. At the conclusion of the story, she regains her powers of speech.

Borges' scholars—and in one sense all his protagonists belong to this class—embark on a quest for meaning that initially produces an expectation of certainty. The strategy of his stories is to enmesh these figures in a maze of ambivalence and ambiguity. The labyrinth comes to represent the ultimate meanings of life, scholarship, and history, and is finally transformed into an image of the symbolic workings and power of language itself. As the sinologist Stephen Albert comments on the riddle of Ts'ui Pen in one of Borges' most famous stories, a governor "learned in astronomy, in astrology and in the tireless interpretation of the canonical books, chess player, famous poet and calligrapher—he abandoned all this in order to compose a book and a maze . . . a labyrinth of symbols . . . an invisible labyrinth of time." The problem Ts'ui Pen solves is that of creating an infinite book. "I had questioned myself about the ways in which a book can be infinite. I could think of nothing other than a cyclic volume, a circular one. A book whose last page was identical with the first, a book which had the possibility of continuing indefinitely." Self-referential, this book is an infinite labyrinth because it realizes the potential force of language as a system that can enact all meanings simultaneously. Albert recognizes this in a flash of insight:

> These conjectures diverted me; but none seemed to correspond, not even remotely, to the contradictory chapters of Ts'ui Pen. In the midst of this perplexity, I received from Oxford the manuscript you have examined. I lingered, naturally, on the sentence: *I leave to the various futures (not to all) my garden of forking paths.* Almost instantly, I understood: "the garden of forking paths" was the chaotic novel; the phrase "the various futures (not to all)" suggested to me the forking in time, not in space. A broad rereading of the work confirmed the theory. In all fictional works, each time a man is confronted with several alternatives, he chooses one and eliminates the others; in the fiction of Ts'ui Pen, he chooses—simultaneously—all of them. He *creates*, in this way, diverse futures, diverse times which themselves also proliferate and fork.[6]

This solution, which functions almost as a mathematical definition of language's power to articulate all aspects of existence, becomes as well the pattern of action in the story. Instead of encountering a particular world in all its fullness—the realistic novel's strength—we glimpse the instrument of world making in play. The story contains all possible variations on itself. Both title and subject, "The Garden of Forking Paths," is the alphabet in whose forms the permutations of meaning in this fictional world are realized. This power of self-realization depends upon its central ambiguity. Albert's comprehension of its power is enacted in the story through our reading of it, parallel to the act of reading central to the functioning of its main characters. Here Borges, like Agnon in *Edo and Enam*, focuses on reading and writing, presenting the world as text, alphabetic labyrinth, library, mystic book, and secret hieroglyph. Both writers' stories are the self-embedding act of releasing their infinite linguistic potential.

In exploring and comparing the theme of language making as it shapes their fictional discourse, we can glimpse the ways in which Agnon and Borges seek to create sacred texts for their respective cultures, charting like the epics of old the spectrum of their cultures' manifold meanings. Both accept their respective traditions as necessary conditions for their work. Agnon and Borges are conscious of the ways in which it depends upon that of others; both writers constantly quote and refer to other writers as part of their fictional strategies, while thereby also proposing ways of reading favorite works and traditions.[7] They accept the mediating functions of their roles, responding to their respective traditions in playfully ironic and oblique ways. Of course, where Agnon is concerned with Israel and Jewish culture, Borges focuses on Argentina and Hispanic culture. The two writers also differ with regard to the point at which each begins his analysis of the symbol-making act of language.

Believing that his Spanish is overwhelmed by clichés and the dead forms of the past, Borges breaks with them while building upon them. Similarly, Agnon cannot merely repeat ancient themes and classical forms but, encountering the modern world in all its complexity, explores the possibility of midrash in his time. Starting from a vision of the literary forms of the past though differing as to the vital force yet resident in them, each writer enlists a crucial principle of structural transformation. As they examine inherited cultural forms, Borges and Agnon uncover models and touchstones for their writing activity. Performing the implicit roles, they move from scholarly detachment to artistic recreation.

Like Borges, Agnon enacts the process of "reading the new in an old text" and skillfully masks old themes in modern dress. Unlike Borges, Agnon does not begin with "the almost infinite world of literature," though he certainly has a wide knowledge of it. Instead his starting point is the world of classical Jewish literature. Against it he plays his representations, which ironically turn out to be old/new versions of ancient themes and tropes, blending many notes into "one unified tone."[8] In effect each writer works out for his own culture a theory of language displaying its historical and modern possibilities; it is an effort to suggest the wholeness of the past and future as continuous aspects of the stream of language, captured in the dialectics of style. Breaking the old forms, Borges' language liberates his world and makes it new and fresh while allowing old interpretations that are transformed in his words, just as Agnon's exegetical sleight of hand makes the modern world as full of potential holiness as the classical text. The two writers conceptualize the process of writing the new sacred texts of their cultures as they contextualize their literary and linguistic traditions through the confrontation with the chaos and unformed experience of the modern world. Thus they explore the idea of culture as language making.

Borges and Agnon establish a linguistic field by means of innumerable references, echoes, and stylistic imitations within which old texts and new worlds encounter each other. This is a dangerous, dialectic activity of mutual confrontation. It is also, however, the very condition by which the old texts can be enacted and put into play, as well as the method by which the new world's possible meanings—perhaps already implicit in received law (and literature) but not yet enacted in history—can be realized. It is for this reason that Borges' tales, like Agnon's, are informed by the idea of commentary—of midrash—as the continuously unfolding process of interpretation.[9]

Agnon's achievement consists in his act of setting his traditional linguistic heritage, the holy tongue of the classical Jewish texts, against the disorder and chaos of modern Jewish life and

Israeli speech. It is an act that both tests the possible force yet resident in the *l'shon hakodesh* and explores the *kedusha*, the holiness, and ceremonial potential of the modern. Agnon does not play current and traditional Hebrew vocabularies, Israeli street slang and mishnaic or biblical tonalities against each other as some Israeli writers do. He allows his language, always carefully and appropriately drawn from a particular source in classic Jewish tradition and highlighted in these terms, its traditional syntax; then in its own terms, he stretches and probes that particular form by having it encounter a contemporary situation with its own modern grammar of action. Most of Agnon's major works focus on the encounter as a testing of the inner vitality of ancient Jewish heritage. That is why so many of his protagonists are scientists, professors, or doctors, who confront situations determined indirectly by the searing events of the last seventy-five years of Jewish history. Then too there is the subtle interplay of the Yiddish rhythms of shtetl speech and mishnaic Hebrew. (In fact, Baruch Hochmann claims that Agnon often writes Hebrew as if it were Yiddish.[10]) But it would be a mistake to look for direct historical referents in Agnon's work. He is too wily for that, creating an oblique method that presents typical events and representative actions in a penumbra of dreams. Several critics have commented on Agnon's characteristic habit of turning a seemingly solid reality into a dream landscape. This is due in large part to the fact that many of his stories articulate psychological interactions not easily apparent in the solid world of facts though indeed terrifyingly real. Furthermore, as Arnold Band points out, these stories are recounted by a narrator in whose consciousness these psychic events often occur. He "embraces all the other characters; they exist because he recreates them in his narrative."[11]

Like so many of the great Jewish writers, Agnon's choice of a literary language came after early experimentation with another. He turned to Hebrew after having tried Yiddish, thus reversing the pattern of choice of Sholom Aleichem, Mendele Mocher Seforim, and even Isaac Bashevis Singer. They opted for the life and play of the vital communal tongue of the European Jewish dispersion; Agnon chose the intellectual, spiritual, and Zionist linguistic context of Hebrew. If Yiddish is present in

Agnon's work, it is there as a trace element rather than as a sub-text.

As a Hebrew writer, Agnon faced the difficulty of creating modern literature in a language that had not been used and spoken by women for more than a thousand years. Turning to erotic themes, he chose to treat them in a broad allegoric and allusive manner, with all the richness made possible by an ancient and intellectually powerful tradition. Bashevis Singer, by contrast, chose to center his fiction quite explicitly on love, dealing with it along a spectrum ranging from the realistic to the metaphysical. With its characteristic mixture of realism and fantasy, Singer's language describes the varied intertwinings of sacred and profane love. His choice of Yiddish, rather than the Hebraic patriarchal tongue of Agnon, commits Singer to a linguistic situation that constantly plays the Hebraic and non-Hebraic resources of Yiddish against each other. Ruth Wisse highlights the process in her comment on a famous Yiddish proverb: "Thou hast chosen us from among the nations—why did you have to pick on the Jews?" Although this is a Yiddish saying, the first part is Hebrew, quoting one of the most prominent phrases of the daily prayers that expresses a central Jewish value. The Yiddish question, she points out, draws attention to the ironic implications of the quoted phrase. "The proverb is in two parts, affirmation and question. The affirmation is in the sacred language, the jibe in the vernacular. The form is dramatic, and the challenge, forcing on the affirmation a meaning contradictory to the ostensible one, is in the traditional Jewish form of aggression, a question."[12] By contrast, Agnon's is a language in which the varied sources are coordinated, and tonalities tend to be more continuous. For him, text—and the ideal model echoes the religious text—is primary, and the effect is always self-conscious and literary. Even in Agnon's stories of Jewish exile, his characters do not speak Yiddish, and the interest of the tale, say in "The Lady and the Peddler," tends to be allegorical.

For the more realistic Singer, character is prior to text. Still, the Hebrew letters of Yiddish are sacred, literally nourishing, like a mother's milk. Thus, in "The Last Demon," the protagonist comments: "I suck on the letters and feed myself." Jewish life in Israel, Agnon's major theme, is absent from Singer's work. Yet, as Edward Alexander notes, "through an ironic reversal of the traditional relationship between Hebrew and Yiddish, the language of the majority of the victims of the Holocaust becomes for Singer the holy tongue of the Jewish people."[13] In *Enemies, a Love Story*, Singer invokes Agnon's high seriousness when Herman Broder meditates on the classical rabbinic text. "He sat over his Gemara, staring at the letters, at the words. These writings were home. On these pages dwelt his parents, his grandparents, all his ancestors." This writing evokes the central values of rabbinic Judaism for this complex character, and for a moment he experiences their sanctity. "These words could never be adequately translated, they could only be interpreted. In context, even a phrase such as 'a woman is for her beauty's sake' had a deep religious significance. It brought to mind the study house, the women's section of the synagogue, penitential prayers, lamentations for martyrs, sacrifice of one's life in the Holy Name." Nevertheless, like a character in the Bible, Herman immediately has to confront the profane world in all its seductiveness. "Not cosmetics and frivolity," he thinks, not pleasure and flirtation, but the inner beauty of women is the meaning of male-female relationships.[14] Once voiced, that pious view gives way to its opposite, and the negative injunction of no cosmetics and frivolity becomes his obsession. Like the plots of his stories, Singer's language blends realism and fantasy in order to render the complicated and contradictory qualities of human experience.

Agnon's narrative method by contrast leads him to create tales that involve us in language as a dream medium in which, as in Borges, all potential can be released. For Agnon and Borges, "consciousness has replaced character." They seduce the reader into expecting the encounter with old-fashioned characters so that by a "complex process of rapport between the author and ourselves we know what to think of them." Anticipating the literary pleasure of writing like Singer's, where author and reader together define "the charmed circle of characterization," we instead find ourselves in a world where explorations of consciousness function to account for the social world, reversing the realistic novel's procedures. "Everyday life becomes a problem for the inquirer who hitherto tacitly accepted the taken-for-granted world as real and valid for everyone. And along with this change in attitude there goes a reassessment of the nature of consciousness and a revaluation of its psychological implications."[15]

Language in its original, poetic sense of making is what is at issue for both Borges and Agnon. For them it is the moving force. Dreaming, and writing-as-dreaming, are the enabling conditions for their inquiries. By these means words become mirrors that reflect the symbol-making activities of their users and thereby define the shapes of consciousness that function as the narrative personae of these tales. Here words (like consciousness) can potentially mirror everything, and the act of writing becomes fateful.

The dream quality of Borges' and Agnon's stories has a peculiar effect. ("After all, writing is nothing more than a guided dream," Borges has stated.[16]) Playing written against spoken language, suggesting a hidden traditional text while expressing a present action, suspending events in a dream medium that undoes chronology, these stories release words from the prison of the printed page into the reader's consciousness. Enacted in the reader's mind, turned into the present action of consciousness, these stories realize their constitutive force. At the climax of *Edo and Enam*, to take one example, Gemula the sleepwalker breaks into song: she chants the ancient texts the scholar has been seeking to decipher. Pronouncing them, she releases their magic and power. For the scholar this is a pygmalion event; mysterious letters and ancient words come alive. The power of these words produces erotic pleasure and leads inexorably to a love-death. The implication is clear: we release a lesser version of this power in the act of reading. The work of Agnon and Borges taps the continuous fountain of language as infinite interpretability. Writing defines and fences in the undifferentiated flow of language, as it is momentarily made concrete in speech.[17] Borges and Agnon remind us that in writing we work with symbols which contain within themselves the possibility, were they properly decoded, of reaching back to that original stream. Thereby Borges and Agnon engage the reader in the search for "the secret of language itself."[18]

These themes are central to two stories—Agnon's "The Face and the Image" and Borges' "Death and the Compass."[19] Like *Edo and Enam*, "The Face and the Image" is a story focused in the dreaming narrator's consciousness. Ostensibly, the story details the interruptions that make it impossible for the narrator to reach his dying mother. Ironically, the telegram informing him of his mother's request that he come to see her is discovered just at the moment he sits down to the great work of writing "down in a book my thoughts about polished mirrors."[20]

From the beginning the narrator expresses an interest in mirrors that dates from his childhood. As this movement of his consciousness unfolds, mirrors and reflection gradually become a metaphor for the action of language and writing. His meditation on polished mirrors reflects his way with words. Like words, "they are flat, and thin, and smooth as ice, and there is nothing inside them." Despite their seeming lack of depth and yet because of their superficiality, they function much as words do, storing "up whatever you put before them, and before them there is no cheating, or partiality, or injustice, or deceit. Whatever you show them, they show you. Mirrors are deserving of praise," for, the narrator says, "they reveal the truth of the world. They do not expunge or amplify, add on or take away—like the truth, which neither adds nor takes away. Therefore I said: I will tell of their virtues and their perfect rectitude."[21]

As the story progresses, it catches this dreamy, naive narrator in the maze of his own words. When his journey to his mother is interrupted—removing him also from his usual writer's work—the symbolic depths of words begin to work upon him. Thus, several pages later, as he awaits the departure of the train that he expects will take him to his mother, he begins to think of himself. No longer flat and thin like a mirror, he deepens his image of himself by meditating upon it, doubling his face by calling up an image of it. "It is good for a man to think about himself a little, and not think what he is always thinking." Like mirrors, his words have heretofore been flat and unselfconscious. Now he will observe himself and his mirroring image. His words begin to grow into self-referential symbols and, as face and image interact, he is caught in this process and gradually forced to scrutinize himself. "I looked at myself and saw myself standing in the station on the carriage step." The figures of the story are doubled repeatedly, face reflected in image as consciousness doubling back upon itself comes to a discovery of its multiple possibilities. With the narrator we enter this maze at the moment he opens the fateful telegram. "For tidiness' sake I took the telegram and laid it on the table. Then I took a knife to open it. At that moment there appeared before me the image of my grandfather, my mother's father, in the year he died, lying in his bed and reading his will all night. His beard was bluish silver and the hair of his beard was not wavy but straight, every single hair hanging by itself and not mingling with the next, but their perfect rectitude uniting them all. I began to calculate how old my grandfather had been when I was born, and how old my mother had been when she bore me, and it turned out that her age today was the same as my grandfather's age at that time, and my age was the same as hers when I was born."[22]

In a startling series of events, the narrator is forced to confront this doubling effect. Unable to travel to his mother without his travel permit, he returns home only to discover that a trivial command to Naomi, his maid, to lock up and take the key with her has left him homeless, since his own key is in the valise he has left on the train. As he looks for the departed Naomi, and seeks a way out of the labyrinth he has made for himself, the narrator meets Naomi's uncle, a carpenter busy fitting a mirror into a door.

The narrator is wearing his writing clothes—old, patched trousers that he thinks makes the carpenter first treat him as of slight consequence. His work clothes are his work words, the classic words of Hebrew, patched and worn yet still useful for meditations on mirrors and truth, but not suitable to the modern world of polished middle-class appearances. These clothes and words are without honor in the modern world, though essential to his work and functional in his study where he can celebrate both mirrors and words. The classical phrases are sufficient for his meditative writer's world, but they cannot perform in the world outside. Furthermore, they are in some sense without content. Though they make it possible for him to praise mirrors and truth abstractly, it is not until they encounter the concrete experience of the world that they can produce the revelation with which the story ends. Amusingly, it is his lack of the proper words of a travel permit, parallel to his lack of a proper traveling outfit, that keeps him from reaching his mother. The entire situation is replete with hidden meanings and demands allegorical interpretation. The sleight of hand of the story depends upon the balance between allegorical and symbolic meanings, which are poised against each other as they are gathered together in the narrator's consciousness.

When the narrator informs the carpenter that he is Naomi's employer, the carpenter and his wife forget his shabby appearance and treat him as befits an important guest. Their sudden hospitality now keeps him from finding Naomi, as well as the key to his home and his travel permit. Invited to partake of the food traditionally made available to an honored guest, the narrator discovers his hunger. At the same time, the feeling that he is missing his mother's burial overwhelms him. The image of her coffin arises before him, as he recollects seeing a coffin borne through a courtyard he passed while en route to the train. He turns and notices his image in the mirror the carpenter has set in the door. Startled, he realizes how flat mirrors and words enable us to see in the round by means of their dialectic force. As the story ends, consciousness hovers between face and image.

> So there I sat against my will, eating and drinking whatever Naomi's relatives gave me. At first I ate and drank against my will, without enjoyment, and then willingly, for hunger had begun to torment me. My house was locked, the key in the valise, the valise in the railway carriage, and the carriage on the way to its destination, and all my thoughts were with my mother; perhaps while I was filling my gullet they were sealing her grave. I turned my head aside so as not to look at what I saw. My image rose before me from the mirror in the wardrobe, which the carpenter had been fixing an hour before. The mirror stared at me face to face reflecting back every movement of the hand and quiver of the lips, like all polished mirrors, which show you whatever you show them, without partiality or deceit. And it, namely the revelation of the thing,

surprised me more than the thing itself, perhaps more than it had surprised me in my childhood, perhaps more than it had ever surprised me before.[23]

The hermeneutic circle of mirrors and words is complete.

The characters in this tale double and reflect each other's function, as they might in a dream, allowing us to experience it along with the narrator. We can try out its multiple meanings as both participants and observers. Thus we move not to a conclusion of plot—the narrator never gets to his mother—but to the reflexive mirroring moment. Mirrors and words, prepared, polished, and set, and the flow of everyday life interrupted, we look into the mirror of words and discover its old/new truths of face and image. This revelatory moment is set in a web of allusions and cryptic hints of quotations that take on surprising new meanings through the encounter with previously unarticulated experience.[24]

We find a similar strategy in "Death and the Compass," one of Borges' classic stories of detection. Like so many of these, it turns on a discovery of and about language which, ironically treated, expands into an image of the general process of creating words, meaning, and reality. In this story the detective discovers what he believes to be the solution of a crime by reading the cabalistic books of the dead man and deciphering their mystic code. The process of seeking is doubled; and Lönnrot, in searching for the Secret Name of God as the solution to the mystery, discovers he has been caught in the labyrinth of words. Though the story concludes with his murder, it is clear that at the same time it begins with that cyclic event: we discover that the process of searching for the Secret Name—part of the maze created by the criminal Scharlach to ensnare Lönnrot—is an unending one. This labyrinth of words becomes an image of our capacity to share in the more-than-human powers of angels and demons as well as in culture as the ceaseless and universal code in which we have our being.

Like Agnon's, this story teases us into finding allegorical meanings. The place names sound mythic—Triste-le-Roy, Hotel du Nord—and the names of the characters as well as their characterizing epithets suggest that they are not individuals but general types who repeat ancient ritual events. Jewish references abound, but they are part of the same iterative process, in which events are doubled and themes are repeated until their very redundancy forces us to look at the process of symbolism and language making by which they are brought into existence.

"To that tower . . . there came on the third day of December the delegate from Podolsk to the Third Talmudic Congress, Doctor Marcel Yarmolinsky, a gray-bearded man with gray eyes. We shall never know whether the Hotel du Nord pleased him; he accepted it with the ancient resignation which had allowed him to endure three years of war in the Carpathians and three thousand years of oppression and pogroms."[25] As the process of detection unfolds, we become aware of the narrator's presence. At one point he is beside Lönnrot eagerly seeking the solution to the mystery; he loses himself in the delight of describing the ambiguities of a place or situation; he marvels at what he cannot know, or tells us everything as if the story were his own. This narrative voice is in tension with the dramatic portions of the story, although it is clear that the narrator is self-consciously playing all the roles. In effect, the story deals with the process of artistic creation as a labyrinth-making activity, in which the narrator embeds himself at the same moment that he expresses it. By this process the narrator reveals some of the same wiliness as Agnon's persona in "The Face and the Image." Each speaker fills a symbol-making role as well as the symbolic role he plays in the tale.

Agnon draws upon classical Jewish sources to define this situation, and adds to it themes and tonalities from the great masters of European literature, as Borges draws upon similar classic sources while referring to the long Spanish perspectivist tradition from Cervantes to Unamuno. Their confluence becomes clear when Lönnrot answers self-consciously a suggestion of police inspector Treviranus. The dead man, Treviranus claims, was killed because he was mistaken for the Tetrarch of Galilee who "owns the finest sapphires in the world." That is a possible but uninteresting solution, Lönnrot responds: "You'll reply that reality hasn't the least obligation to be interesting. And I'll answer you that reality may avoid that obligation but that hypotheses may not. In the hypothesis that you propose, chance intervenes copiously. Here we have a dead rabbi; I would prefer a purely rabbinical explanation, not the imaginary mischances of an imaginary robber." Like a sensible policeman, Treviranus replies, "I'm not interested in rabbinical explanations, I am interested in capturing the man who stabbed this unknown person." What Treviranus seeks to keep separate—world and words—Lönnrot insists on linking. "Not so unknown. Here are his complete works."[26] Thus Lönnrot is launched on his course of reading, that is, of world making, from which his life and death issue.

Though the books in Yarmolinsky's library belong to him, they are not only his, for they are no more than personal copies of classical Jewish cabalistic works. Yarmolinsky like Lönnrot is merely one of the avatars of this cyclic activity of language making, one of the figures in the dance, as are Borges and Agnon. Treviranus comments that he has no time for musty volumes since he is too busy to waste it on Jewish superstitions. Lönnrot's murmured answer—"Maybe the crime belongs to the history of Jewish superstitions"—is triumphantly vindicated by succeeding events. After all, as the editor of the *Yidische Zaitung* comments shyly, Christianity belongs "to the history of Jewish superstitions" (note the doubling here). And then one of the policemen finds in Yarmolinsky's typewriter the cryptic message, "The first letter of the Name has been uttered."[27]

It is clear that Lönnrot's quest will thus articulate the very nature of that time Treviranus refuses to waste. Furthermore, when we note that the letters of God's name have been uttered in the scattered messages and clues that follow like punctuation marks in the story, we realize that the act of reading and decoding a text is being imagined for us as it creates reading (and writing) time. Here reader, narrator, and writer join in the complicitous acts of making, of consciousness, and of literature. Thus, like Agnon's, Borges' stories eschew the realistic idea of harmony, completeness, and self-sufficiency in favor of commentary on—which is also revelation of—the nature of things and words. For both writers this is a cyclic and unending process, individual as well as impersonal, new yet always old. As writers, they are inscribed in it as they write out the unending permutations of the Name—not only of God but of Language.

7
Language Rules

Releasing the energies of tradition into their modern writing, Agnon and Borges explored a classical western aesthetic. If the secret of their work focuses on this effort to nurture a renaissance of the western cultural enterprise at its geographic margins, in finding new resources by exploring ancient linguistic texts and values, the problem confronting contemporary writers is structurally different. For them the question is not revival but resurrection, as they seek for new life in languages soaked in blood and ashes.

At the limits of language brought about by the death of its nurturing community of speakers and users, Jewish writers explore a different aesthetic characterized not by inspiration but expiration.[1] The challenge facing them is how Jewish writing can continue in the twentieth century when two of the languages of its greatest achievements have been silenced by modern history. If few Jews now write in Yiddish, almost none is active in German. How rich a set of worlds has thereby been closed off we can surmise simply by remembering what even the remnants of those who do work in Yiddish and German have managed.

It is possible that a linguistic displacement of the cultural values the Jews articulated in these languages may occur. Other languages may manage to carry forward the values and identities set in these two. If we have glimpsed some of the ways in which Yiddish has infiltrated and interrupted English, it is worth considering what the situation of German is and might become. My question is directed toward psychology as well as linguistics and focuses on the characteristic human types who stamped these languages in their image as it imprinted itself upon their being. How, we may ask, will these be available to the Jews, and through them to general cultural use, in other linguistic forms and codes. Or are they now a finished book— completed because so abruptly truncated?

It is understandable why the work of recent Jewish writers has been open to the pressure of Yiddish rather than German, though we must admit that both cultural achievements were truly astounding. There are still some writers whose work is accented with the inflections of the German-Jewish symbiosis. Such translation and displacement continues in particular among an older generation of Israeli writers working in Hebrew and Americans—German-Jewish refugees—writing in English. Though much will thereby be irretrievably lost, it is doubtful that either will set a direction for younger generations. That possibility depends in part upon what happens to non-Jewish German writers, as they confront their terrible and catastrophic history.

How to deal with the massive linguistic disturbances of Nazi-Deutsch is central to the work of contemporary German writers.[2] They must use a language that was reduced to the service of a monstrous ideology and exploited so thoroughly for the purposes of totalitarianism that it "found its deepest and most characteristic expression not in the propaganda speeches of Hitler or Goebbels against 'international Jewry' and 'Bolshevism' but in the common usage of the people." Nazi Germany was abandoned by most of its serious writers, who sought asylum abroad while its leaders engaged in parody of its classics and perversion of the values of its finest literary traditions. Their regime "effectively invalidated language and made it forfeit its usefulness as the primary means of social and cultural discourse."[3] This is the secret gnawing at the heart of contemporary German writing, confronted among others by Heinrich Böll, who explores its dimensions in the post-Nazi generation.

There is a jolting moment early in Böll's novel *Group Portrait with Lady*, when words fail the narrator, "the Au." as he calls himself. He has been assiduously gathering material and interviewing witnesses for his report on "the female protagonist," one Leni Pfeiffer, née Gruyten. She is the proprietor of a sleazy rooming house inhabited by foreigners (mostly Basques and Turks) who occupy themselves with the garbage collection of a representative German city north of the Rhine. Culling background material from newspapers and books, he draws up his report on the causes of her present demeaning status. The narrator has reached the winter of 1940 at the point in her life when Leni's cousin and lover Erhard and her brother Heinrich have been executed for sabotage and espionage. Here is a crisis presumably intense enough to make the narrator grope for words, for these two young men, duly sworn soldiers, have opposed the might of the Third Reich. Nevertheless, it is discussed, elaborated, noted without a break in the report, and dismissed with a comment: "It seems pretty German to me, what those two boys did," (notes Lotte Hoyser, daughter of the man who is Leni's father's assistant in the fortifications business). Lotte adds that she considers the implications of their act "symbolllism, if you like, with three l's please."[4]

Even puns on his own name cannot help the Au. when it comes to describing Leni's feelings at this point in her life. Language and experience alike fail him, and he is reduced to consulting an encyclopedia. "Since the Au. neither is in a position to meditate on tears nor considers himself suited to do so," he notes, information on their origin, and "chemical and physical composition, can best be obtained from a handy reference work." By way of describing Leni's emotions, the Au. seems only able to follow through the various crossreferences in the encyclopedia. When he reads, "Weeping—like—Laughter, form of expression in time of crisis, i.e., of grief, emotion, anger, or happiness; *psychologically* . . . an attempt at mental or emotional release," his only response is to look up Laughter; Happiness, which is not listed; Bliss, which is defined; Pain; and Suffering—"It (S.) 'is felt by a person with a severity proportionate to his quality of life and to the sensitivity of his nature.' " From this point on in the novel, the Au., having completed the "definition of concepts," refers to them by their capital letters alone.[5]

The narrative stratagem is to protect subjective life against the clichés that reduce it, an important procedure since Leni, like her brother and cousin, stands in opposition to the dominant culture—at the time of the Nazis or in the present of the novel, which is set in Europe of the 1960s and 1970s. Like her brother and cousin, Leni has committed a treasonable action—she took a Soviet prisoner of war as her lover, had a son by him, and, after the war, lived openly with him. Furthermore, after his death she participated in communist rallies. Recently she has taken a Turkish boarder as her lover. One of the kindest phrases by which she is referred to in the neighborhood is Communist whore. Böll is trying to elicit the secret life of these antifascist Germans. His report is an account of how they managed then, and continue today, to maintain their values in the face of overwhelming opposition.

The failure of language with which the Au. is confronted, like the failure of narrative itself that fragments his report into episodic accounts of the evidence, is more than a literary problem for Böll. He is implicated in it as Au.—as a character in a novel that increasingly involves him in highly suspicious activities and enmeshes him so that he too undergoes all those emotions he has attempted to define with the help of "the seven volume encyclopedia put out by a controversial publisher, 1966 edition." Furthermore, Böll has dedicated the book to Leni, her Soviet lover Boris, and their son Lev, so that the borders between fiction and real life are blurred. Leni, who loves to play Schubert and quote Yeats, is the Lady who not only endows the Au. with the ability to comprehend the Holocaust, but also bestows upon him the personal happiness with which the novel concludes. Finally, her life and person in which he becomes so intimately involved grants him the novelistic sine qua non: the possibility of speaking authentically and truly about what is unspeakable.

The Au.'s task with Leni, then, is that of reconstructing language to make it possible for him to grasp the recent history of Germany and Europe. Böll's novel displays the precision we associate with the best modern critical histories. The Au. sifts through materials in search of evidence that will enable him to reconstruct the latent history of Germany, which is in all things a contradiction of the official Nazi version. He uncovers a world of secret Jews masquerading as Germans; of fascist activity by ordinary Germans, which they will later deny with typical bad faith; of an existence gradually shrinking in material and spiritual possibilities until, under the impact of incessant bombing by the Allies, it becomes a version of concentration-camp life: meaningless work, emptied people, an absurd world, with death as its only release. As a nun comments offhandedly to the Au., "Since I assume you have some small measure of insight into the dialectics of motivation I needn't explain that if one wishes to save a person from concentration camp one is more or less obliged to hide that person under concentration-camp conditions."[6] At times the novel reads like a parable exploring the ways in which these Germans cope with the experience into which Nazism thrust Germany while obliquely glancing at the murder of European Jewry.

Focusing on the problem of the destruction of language, which is to say of meaning, Böll traces the ways in which existence has shriveled. He finds in Leni the imaginative effort to make a life for herself, despite the all-encompassing meaninglessness that is the vacuous cultural ether of existence even in the German present. Her effort is of necessity secret and secretive: in her relationship with the Soviet prisoner Boris, a fellow worker in the wreath-making factory, she wrests life from the very jaws of death. They express their love in the cemetery adjacent to the factory, during the free time afforded by the Allied air raids, when a mausoleum vault offers them more than an air-raid shelter. Their son Boris is begotten and born in the one they have made into a home. Confronting the omnipotence of death, Leni constructs her life. Even after the war, as the German miracle of rebuilding and prosperity is in full swing, death is everywhere in the refusal to face the Holocaust. It is most apparent in the cliché-ridden language that masks the organized violence of authority. When they attempt to deny Leni her house, a splendid farcical scene ensues. The court officials are outwitted, baffled by Leni's words and the actions of a ragtag group of conspirators, among whom the despised Turks and Basques figure prominently.

The Au. confronts the clichés of technocracy and the violence of supposed progress when he interviews the Hoyser children, successful businessmen who want to evict their aunt Leni. They attempt to buy him off, but he is repulsed by their technological doubletalk that recalls Orwell's doublethink. He joins in the successful counterattack that secures for Leni the right to continue her effort to make a meaningful world for herself, as she sets up house with her Turkish lover, Mehmet Sahin, and proudly bears his child. It is at this moment in Leni's life that her addiction to Yeats's poems makes its triumphant reappearance, as she sings his famous song.[7] For her too there is more enterprise in "walking naked" than in clothing herself with the old embroidered mythologies and their corrupted words. Leni dismisses those language rules that have rendered the Au. speechless, teaching him by her example the ways in which the process of language making makes possible the creation of a vital and dynamic reality.

Böll confronts one of the central issues of modern writing. To what extent can he use a language appropriated and remade by modern incarnations of evil to describe reality? The modern writer discovers that realism as the trust in language is no longer readily available. He must find a way to rediscover the sources of language and like Böll explore its possibilities in order to find a way of linking it to an external world of monstrous actions. In this situation, the novel cannot have the sequencing, order, and flow of realistic narratives; surrealist montage, cubist collage, and existential parable are the only appropriate possibilities. Remaking narration and language, Böll discovers the realities of the modern world.

Any consideration of language and its making of meaning as thorough-going and serious as this, especially when written by a German, recalls Arendt's famous thesis about Eichmann.[8] It is the same issue confronted by Sammler in Bellow's novel.[9] There too the debasement of language is one of the ways in which the Holocaust makes its pressure felt. Understandably this question of language and cliché, on which Arendt has focused in her study of Eichmann, is a major concern of all writers, striking as it does at the very material and the medium of their work. What is especially interesting here is the way in which Böll offers a criticism close to Bellow's. Several of Böll's characters, notably Kurt and Werner Hoyser, exemplify the meaninglessness of lan-

guage and speak in clichés parallel to Eichmann's—not just because they are banal in their evil but because that banality is the
measure of their bad faith. Böll proposes in effect that what
Arendt saw as Eichmann's cliché-ridden mentality, which in
good bureaucratic fashion obeyed all the rules—even the language rules that cloaked the destruction of European Jewry in
terms like Final Solution—was a self-conscious, knowing act of
evil.

At the point of death, traditionally the moment in which a
man fully understands the meaning of his life, Eichmann "began
by stating emphatically that he was a *Gottgläubiger*, to express
in common Nazi fashion that he was no Christian. He then proceeded, 'After a short while, gentlemen, we shall all meet again.
Such is the fate of all men. Long live Germany, long live Argentina, long live Austria. I shall not forget them.' " If we had expected Eichmann to crack and drop the role he had been playing
at the moment of his death—Arendt's implicit comparison—in
order to sum up the true meaning of his life, we would be offering him the possibilities of heroism and truth telling. Instead,
Eichmann affirms that his pretentious words, like those of the
Hoysers', are his true being, not an ironic pose. "In the face of
death, he had found the cliché used in funeral oratory. Under
the gallows, his memory played him the last trick; he was
'elated' and he forgot that this was his own funeral. It was as
though in those last minutes he was summing up the lessons that
this long course in human wickedness had taught us—the lesson
of the fearsome, word-and-thought-defying banality of evil."[10]
The language in which he sentimentalizes his own death is the
same he has used to hide from the meaning of his murderous
career. In proclaiming his inability to think—about himself, his
actions, his life—he defines his words and life as that of a murdering bureaucrat. He has become one with the reality he made
for himself: his language encompasses the shrunken, pitiful
(even though it was pitiless) world in which he lived. It is even
less of a meaningful world than the concentration-camp realms
over which he ruled. In them, as we see in Böll's novel, the
struggle to find, make, and cherish meanings still existed.
Imagination and utopian quests—the will to be—were still possible, despite the horror of existence. Leni and the Jews have

lived even in dying—an experience the Hoysers, like Eichmann, have been denied. To confront either is to enter their language. Eichmann was, incidentally, something of a linguist, and could speak perfect Yiddish—a fact that perhaps explains why he "felt he understood 'Jewish' psychology."[11]

It is worth examining Eichmann's German, as Arendt has done, in some detail, for it was dominated by rules whose function was anaesthetic: to insulate its users from encountering the meaning of their action and speech. In Nazi Germany language rules dominated all discourse connected with the machinery of the state. Committed totally to the war against the Jews, even to losing the fight against the Allies, bureaucratic jargon became the medium of German life. "All the correspondence referring to killing Jews was subject to rigid language rule and except for the reports of the *Einsatzgruppen* (the killing squads) it is rare to find documents in which such bald words as extermination, liquidation or killing occur. The prescribed code names for killing were final solution, evacuation and special treatment, deportation, change of residence and labor in the east." Some of these names had meaning, since Jews were often temporarily settled in ghettos and a percentage of them were occasionally used for labor; slight changes in language rules were even made. Thus "a high official in the foreign office once proposed that in all correspondence with the Vatican the killing of Jews be called the radical solution for certain political reasons." Even very important individuals in this whole machinery rarely talked in uncoded language, and never when they were able to be recorded or in the presence of stenographers. These language rules "proved of enormous help in maintaining order and sanity in the various widely diversified services [of the German State] whose cooperation was essential in this matter." In effect, "the very term 'language rule' (*Sprachregelung*) was itself a code name," referring to what in ordinary language we would call a lie.[12]

Finding another name for murder, the entire apparatus of the Third Reich insulated itself from the meaning of its actions. When "Eichmann was sent to show the Theresienstadt ghetto to International Red Cross representatives from Switzerland—he received, together with his orders, his language rule, which in this instance consisted of a lie about a non-existent typhus epidemic in the concentration camp of Bergen-Belsen, which the gentlemen also wanted to visit." The effect of this language system was not to keep "these people ignorant of what they were doing, but to prevent them from equating it with their old normal knowledge of murder and lies" and allow them to compartmentalize their minds. "Eichmann's great susceptibility to catch words and stock phrases combined with his incapacity for ordinary speech, made him, of course, an ideal subject for 'language rules.' "[13] They had two functions: to protect oneself from admitting the enormity of what one was doing; and to maintain order and sanity and let the machine function smoothly, serving as a public mask. All of these are thematically present in Böll's novel. He too is horrified by the way the self becomes the mask, official clichés the structure of thinking.

When Eichmann went to visit the killing center at Treblinka, he almost fainted. He tells us in his memoirs that he didn't know what it was to be used for, since he arrived before the death factory opened. The description of its workings—"the engine of a Russian submarine will be set to work and the gasses will enter this building and the Jews will be poisoned" struck Eichmann as "monstrous. I am not so tough as to be able to endure something of this sort without any reaction . . . If today I am shown a gaping wound, I can't possibly look at it, I am that type of person so that very often I was told that I couldn't become a doctor. I still remember how I pictured the thing to myself and then I became physically weak as though I had lived through some great agitation—such things happen to everybody and it left behind a certain inner trembling."[14] A word count of this passage reveals its most important word to be "I": Eichmann spent his time thinking of himself, sentimentalizing his identity by exaggerating his own feelings to keep from seeing the reality he was helping to constitute. Though he can "picture the thing," and the image makes him weak, his refusal to confront its actuality is a willful denial of its meaning. Like so many "good" Germans, he refused either to think or speak of the unspeakable. Not that words failed him—he always had a ready supply at hand, but they were premanufactured, predigested, so to speak, to fit every occasion.

Böll captures a similar moment when Hoyser father and sons explain why they must evict Leni, a fact whose meaning their language keeps them from acknowledging. "Is it our fault if today each square yard is worth three hundred and fifty marks? If we take into consideration certain—as I believe—temporary inflationary trends, you might say the figure was actually five hundred." And further on: "so that you won't think we're prudish or old-fashioned, or not progressive, the point here is not the lovers, not even the Turks or the Italians or the Greeks—the point is that the property is showing a profit of almost 65 percent less than it should . . . And the last straw was the fact that she was charging the unfurnished rate for furnished rooms; and that, mind you, was nothing as harmless as some anarchistic-Communist experiment—that was undermining the market."[15] They too sentimentalize the situation and focus the problem in their own concerns. Like Eichmann, they cannot recognize the presence of the other—even when that person is their aunt. Here Böll uses the family relationship to underline the intertwined connections of German and Jew which yet did not make the Jew recognizable as a human being by the Nazis.

Like the Hoysers, Eichmann had a flair for exit lines. His language asks for psychological examination by someone "wise enough to understand that the horrible can be not only ludicrous but outright funny." Some of the comedy cannot be conveyed in English because it lies in Eichmann's heroic fight with the German language, which invariably defeats him. Arendt highlights some of his incredible mistakes when he talks of "'winged words' (*geflügelte Worte*, a German colloquialism for famous quotes from the classics)." When he uses them he means "*Redensarten* or *Schlagworte*, phrases or slogans." It is a consistent slip of the tongue, a habit and structure of his mind. When the confused judges asked him what he was referring to, Eichmann finally said, in an apologetic tone, "Officialese (*Amtssprache*) is my only language."[16]

John Stuart Mill makes the general point, of which Eichmann is a particular example, with characteristic subtlety, modesty, and precision, in ways that echo Böll's presentation of the fascist habit of mind that afflicts the Hoyser brothers. "In England I had seen and continued to see many of the opinions of my

youth obtain general recognition, and many of the reforms and
institutions for which I had through life contended either ef-
fected or in course of being so," but these changes were "attended with much less benefit to human well-being than I
should formerly have anticipated." The result "was little improvement in that which all real improvement in the lot of man-
kind depends on—their intellectual and moral state: and it
might even be questioned if the various causes of deterioration
which had been at work in the meanwhile had not more than
counterbalanced the tendencies to improvement." It is not simply a matter of the correct views. "I had learnt from experience
that many false opinions may be exchanged for true ones without in the least altering the habits of mind of which false opinions are the result."[17] What is at stake, then, is not just a matter
of the right vocabulary or the right sentence structure, but the
ways in which we think about and use words. It is not surprising to find that destruction of western culture, which culmi-
nated in the Holocaust, at work in language, for the discarding
of values that was perhaps the cause and certainly the result of
the destruction of European Jewry is basically a voiding of language. Six million is a number, not a meaning, and its six zeros
represent graphically the semantic hole burned in the traditions
and languages of the West by the catastrophe of Nazism.

Jewish tradition has its own habits in dealing with this link
between language and value. Facing disaster, it is voiced most
forcefully and notably in a story like that of Rabbi Hanina Ben
Teradion, one of the martyrs at the hands of the Romans who,
wrapped in the Torah scrolls, told his disciples, "I see the parchment consumed by fire, but the letters of the Scriptures are flying aloft."[18] Jewish tradition in its rabbinic incarnation nurtured
the language and thereby the meanings and values of Hebrew
through two thousand years of exile. Thus the Talmud tells us
that he who speaks Hebrew is assured of a place in the world to
come. Paradoxically, Hebrew was to become a flaming brand,
a language blown to the white heat of Israel's revived nationhood immediately after the destruction of meaning and language wrought by German fascism.

What Böll is getting at when he elicits the world of the ordinary German as a concentration camp is the death of meaning
for the Germans and the evacuation of reality as they pervert

their language. As the war goes against them, these average and even representative Germans become desperate and despairing. Only Leni—selected how ironically and appropriately as the most German girl of her class by the Aryan school inspectors in the late 1930s, can function to find meaning—in short, to live. At the end of the war as the Allies approach, Böll records incident after incident of a crazed soldiery. Though their cause is hopeless, the Nazi soldiers continue to kill, finally murdering all those in their own camp who make the slightest gesture of surrender. In so doing, they are affirming the emptiness of their own lives, the death-in-life of their existence. They have made death into the only meaning of their world, the only messiah they can hope for.

Obsessed with "purification," committed to emptying their country—and later the world—of "alien" elements and non-Aryan racial strains, the Nazis created a system that ended up feeding on itself. Amos Oz, the contemporary Israeli writer, observes a similar process at work in the Jew-hating crusades of medieval Christendom, and others have commented on the similar dynamic permeating Spain after the Catholic reconquest if not before. In Böll's novel, purification is an important theme: how to deal with one's bodily wastes is central to Leni's education in the convent. Böll thereby focuses attention on the link between the body and its political analogue, offering us a way of comprehending the meaning of words like *Judenrein*: they signify the end of Yiddish and German Jewish culture physically as well as linguistically. In destroying both, the Nazis were attempting to rewrite their history as part of their effort to reinvent themselves as Aryans. Ironically, they had to untwist the strands of Yiddish and the contributions of German Jewry from culture and language in order to carry out the work of purification. They had to destroy two urban subcultures crucial to their own. Having defined the Jew as central to the modern culture they despised, yet relied on as the vehicle of their greatness, the Nazis adapted the physical configuration in which the Jews had thrived—and precisely for that reason had come to appear as the beneficiaries of urbanization and modernization—in order to destroy them. If they were to be death factories, the concentration camps had first to be made ghettos by the Nazis.

What the Nazis had designated to themselves as cities of

death became through the efforts of their unwilling inhabitants concentrations of cultural achievement, learning, and resistance maintained to the very end in the face of the most unspeakably inhuman conditions. Auschwitz became a gross parody of modern life: its inhabitants were turned from craftsmen, professionals, businessmen, artists, housewives, and communal coordinators into laborers, as if Walter Benjamin's analysis of repetition as the condition of modern work had been accepted and then revalued as good, insofar as Jews were concerned.

Nazi language was the crucial lever of the machinery of humiliation. In *The Last of the Just* André Schwarz-Bart captures the situation in rendering the moment when a new arrival at Auschwitz trips. A German steps forward with an attack dog. Addressing the animal, he shouts, "Man, destroy that dog."[19] His words functioned as well to keep the guard from understanding his own participation in mass murder and insulated him from his guilt. Resistance to the Nazis thus meant confronting their power to destroy language and instituting wherever possible those practices that might keep its meaning-making potential and its symbolizing possibilities alive. It is one of the ways in which the mere fact of recording these experiences became an act of witness.

Yiddish as well as German-Jewish culture emerged as emancipation freed the Jews to enter European life. Both were devised by people breaking free of a confined existence that had for centuries been imposed upon them. The enabling condition for secular Jewish culture was participation in the urban life of Europe. Migrating to the city in the middle of the nineteenth century from the shtetl, the Jews sought metropolitan possibilities. As citizens imbued with the energies of their recent liberation, they helped to endow the new urban civilization with cosmopolitan qualities.

To dwell for a moment on the German-Jewish situation is to encounter a culture and literature created by city immigrants and their urban children, many of whom became famous for their abilities as writers in their adopted tongue. It was natural for Franz Kafka to write in German. His father had embraced the German culture of Prague, which to most of its Jewish inhabitants seemed *"the* secular culture."[20] A newcomer to the city that had once been a major center of Jewish life, Hermann Kafka moved there from the village in southern Bohemia in which he had been born and that had served as the base from which he carried out his forays as itinerant peddler and trader. In Prague he married, and with the help of his wife's parents set up a shop selling fancy cloth and lace. There he prospered. Though nominally a liberal Jew, he hardly concerned himself with his heritage, participating with his secularizing compatriots in the process that led in the course of a few decades to the ousting of Rashi by Schiller from the consciousness of the Jews. His son, who was born in the medieval heart of Prague, would benefit from a European and German destiny. A little more than fifty years later, neither father nor son would be alive to join three daughters and sisters in Auschwitz where they were murdered.

If the nightmare of Kafka's fictional world focuses on the individual's need for recognition, the secret of his identity, then this is surely linked as well to the intensity of Prague, a city of three colliding cultures. Kafka's German originated in a small "linguistic group in a predominantly Czech-speaking town. 'Prager-Deutsch' was narrow in vocabulary, uncertain in idiom, with no roots in a living local language, a papery German, coloured by pidgin-Czech and traces of Yiddish."[21] Immigrants and marginal men choose their language to indicate their affiliation and alliance rather than out of a natural or conditioned response. Their identity is informed by the choice of language, and the strain of choosing is often present in their usage.[22] This problematic is part of the linguistic tension of Kafka's writing, directing him to develop a "clarified literary language" from a "poverty-stricken" medium. In Kafka's inquiry into the idiosyncrasies of Yiddish in his remarkable lecture, as Wolfgang Fischer notes, "he is paying homage to the lost dialect of his soul," echoed in his diary entry of 1914: "What have I in common with the Jews? I have hardly anything in common with myself."[23]

Encountering the Yiddish Theater of Vilna in the winter of 1911-12, Kafka was stunned by the vitality of Eastern European Yiddish culture. (Weizmann records a similar experience of Herzl's a decade earlier.[24]) He was prompted by his response to organize a poetry reading for the Reform Jewish burghers of his town, composing and delivering his lecture on the Yiddish language at that time. The intensity that informs his talk, like the love and care with which he comments on this Jewish tongue, suggests he may even have considered the possibility of writing in Yiddish, or at least like Heine of using some of its phrases in his work. Later, especially under the impact of his love for Dora Diamant, he must have considered the Zionist possibility of writing in Hebrew. We know that he studied it diligently.

His fascination with Yiddish expresses itself as the central paradox of his lecture: related to German, the native Jewish language is accessible to German speakers, but impossible for the secularized Jews of Prague to comprehend because of its rootedness in Jewish culture. "Before we come to the first poems by our Eastern Jewish poets," Kafka comments, "I should like, ladies and gentlemen, just to say something about how much more Yiddish you understand than you think." The intonation of his words carries us into a world that forces Yiddish upon consciousness. Kafka speaks as if the mother tongue were a character in one of his stories, as his German words reveal him "trying to perform some impossible therapy" and fill up "a deep flaw that runs through his confidence in the world's reality."[25] Bear in mind, he comments to his audience, "that apart from what you know there are active in yourselves forces and associations . . . that enable you to understand Yiddish intuitively." Relinquishing the effort to maintain their identity as modern Germans and Prague burghers, these Jews may return to their community of origin through the vehicle of Yiddish, the *mameloshen*, just as the narrator does in Kazin's *A Walker in the City* in returning to the Brownsville of his youth. Kafka continues:

> Then you will come to feel the true unity of Yiddish, and so strongly that it will frighten you, yet it will no longer be fear of Yiddish but of yourselves. You would not be capable of bearing this fear on its own, but Yiddish instantly gives you, besides, a self-confidence that can stand up to this fear and is even stronger than it is. Enjoy this self-confidence as much as you can! But then, when it fades

out, tomorrow and later—for how could it last, fed only on the memory of a single evening's recitations!—then my wish for you is that you may also have forgotten the fear. For we did not set out to punish you.[26]

Language, value, and culture, Yiddish in these words is also family. Encouraging his fellow Jews to relax into their past, Kafka shows them the way to recapture their wholeness, in an implicit therapeutic model for conceiving the relations between modernity, writing, and the Jewish people.

It is worth noting that the first of the poems recited after Kafka's lecture was "Die Grine" by Morris Rosenfeld, about new immigrants, known as greenhorns, just come to America. Rosenfeld was a famous New York Yiddish poet, whom Hutchins Hapgood came to know and discussed in *The Spirit of the Ghetto*. "A Singer of Labor," Hapgood called him, writing "in the universal Yiddish" as a thorough "representative, one might say victim even, of the modern spirit."[27] In his work, Yiddish found a modern American voice.

Kafka's Jewish habits leave traces in the urban nightmare of his work, which portrays complex and often paranoid responses by his characters to an ultimately threatening modern world. Although his language bears none of the marks of the Yiddish-inflected qualities of style of other modern Jewish writers, the crisp German of some of his major stories, such as "The Judgment," echoes the complex associations and terminology of the Reform German prayer book. If he camouflages the Jewish sources of his writing, perhaps this also makes it possible for Kafka thereby to "universalize and objectify certain emotions which had . . . seemed private, even solipsistic."[28] Part of the enigma of his work includes the profound interest in Yiddish, whose history he discussed with such intensity and keen insight in 1912, just as he began to write his first great works. Kafka's grotesque and comic images of the surreal city have reminded many readers of Sholom Aleichem's portrayal of catastrophe.[29] And they have remarked as well how Kafka found it natural to use a map of the psyche much like Freud's as a chart for his imaginings of the realities of urban (and Jewish) life.[30]

In contrast to Kafka's embrace, Freud's response to the

Yiddish-speaking Jews of Eastern Europe who flooded into Vienna around the First World War was a mixture of sympathy, for their plight as refugees, and shock. Unlike others of his countrymen in the capital of the soon to be dismembered Hapsburg empire, he did not avoid them in order to evade identification as a Jew by the Austrians. The greater turmoil for Freud came some twenty years later with the news that *Totem and Taboo* was to be translated into Hebrew, and is expressed in his proposed preface for that edition. His response surely parallels what Kafka would have thought had he been alive in the 1960s when his work was translated into Hebrew in Israel.

No reader of the Hebrew version of the book, Freud says, "will find it easy to put himself in the emotional position of an author who is ignorant of the language of holy writ, who is completely estranged from the religion of his fathers—as well as from every other religion—and who cannot take a share in nationalist ideals, but who has yet never repudiated his people, who feels that he is in his essential nature a Jew and who has no desire to alter that nature." Sharing with Kafka a deep commitment to German culture, Freud also understands the ways in which he is still a Jew. "If the question were put to him: 'Since you have abandoned all these common characteristics of your countrymen, what is there left to you that is Jewish?' he would reply: 'A very great deal, and probably its very essence.' He could not now express that essence clearly in words; but some day, no doubt, it will become accessible to the scientific mind." Freud's response of muted elation leads him to a statement about the place of science in the modern Jewish spirit of Israel. Kafka might have said the same about literature. It "is an experience of a quite special kind for such an author when a book of his is translated into the Hebrew language and put into the hands of readers for whom that historic idiom is a living tongue: a book, moreover, which deals with the origin of religion and morality, though it adopts no Jewish standpoint and makes no exceptions in favour of Jewry. The author hopes, however, that he will be at one with his readers in the conviction that unprejudiced science cannot remain a stranger to the spirit of the new Jewry."[31] Between them, Kafka's lecture on Yiddish and Freud's preface to the Hebrew edition of *Totem and Taboo* define the boundaries and Jewish possibilities of the German culture they shared.

Was it an illusion, we may ask? Were there always two Germanies—that of Schiller and Goethe poised against Hitler and Goebbels, two German traditions, even two languages? As Peter Gay comments, "for most German Jews, wherever their exile, however much they had undergone, the Jewish-German symbiosis was not a mirage that finally lifted but a reality that had been wantonly destroyed."[32] Nevertheless, the roots of barbarian Nazism were intertwined with humanist Germany, and the former would strangle the latter as a result of the peculiar concatenations of German and European history in the twentieth century.

For the modern Jew, the choice of language was fateful. It was in the nature of modernity to offer him the possibility of choice, as it was perhaps characteristic as well that later it would help the Nazis destroy him in recompense for his effort to participate in its enterprise. "When, with Moses Mendelssohn in the eighteenth century, and in the nineteenth with emancipation, German became, not the second language of Germany's Jews, but their first, this shift of priorities engendered a psychological transformation, a transvaluation of identities, that was unprecedented in its scope," Gay comments. "Its crucial importance has not been sufficiently recognized. What makes the modern Jew, everywhere outside Israel and largely even there, radically and permanently different from his ancestors is precisely that his first language is modern Hebrew or French or English or German. What preserves the Jew's separateness in this, our iron age, is far less his ancient religion or some distinct culture than his terrible memories; it is Hitler who has defined the modern Jew and continues to define him from the grave."[33] Despite the effort to become modern, the Jew has learned that his condition in the twentieth no less than the tenth century is exile.

In response to the ethnic mood of American culture in the last two decades, Cynthia Ozick's exploration of the possibilities of Jewish identity in the modern world focuses on the problem of exile. In calling for a new Jewish writing, she seeks a way to recover traditional Jewish culture and make it a vital presence in American Jewish life. She bases her enterprise on a powerful in-

sight into the historical situation, for she knows that, like rabbinic Judaism, Yiddish culture emerged from the Jewish talent
for making a home even within the homelessness of exile. And
yet Ozick is obsessed by the result of that homelessness when it
confronted modernity in the form of the Nazi death machine.
Does it then make sense to seek to rebuild another such home-
away-from-home, she asks? Or is the Zionist possibility the
only real one?

Part of her quarrel with ethnicity results from her acquaintance with the traditional texts and their supporting ideology.
Ozick grew up in a non-Jewish atmosphere, where she was the
only Jewish child in her public school, and perhaps out of that
isolation she sought personal access to its traditions and its
Hebraic high culture. Some of the force of her valuation of tradition results from the individual effort to reconstruct it and regain its mythic power for her characters in the face of the Holocaust. Her story "The Pagan Rabbi" focuses on a passage from
the *Ethics of the Fathers* where the reality of nature is opposed
to the higher reality of the text, and the dramatic confrontation
is between pagan nature worship and Jewish creation of a
higher second nature. In the story, which takes place in a park
in New York, we have an echo of the confrontation Buber and
Rosenzweig proposed as the beginning point for modern Jewish
culture. "The Pagan Rabbi" depends upon the recreation of the
activity of midrash and the reconstruction of the power of ancient texts. Its hero, like the protagonists of the stories of Borges
and Agnon, is someone for whom reading is the world-defining
act.[34]

Ozick does not speak Yiddish; she was not raised on the
lower east side; and she is more at home with the Zionist premises of modern Israel. Thus she gives Israel and, by extension,
Hebrew culture pride of place as the spiritual center of the Jews.
Nevertheless, she argues for the possibility that America may
become another Yavneh, the place where rabbinic Judaism was
invented and articulated after the collapse of Jewish independence under the hammer of Rome. If America is to become such
a Jewish center, and not simply a new version of the tenuous
ground the German Jews inhabited, it would be the result, she
claims, of the historical enrichment of English by Yiddish. Op-

posing the "aesthetic paganism" of the 1960s and the universalism and abstractness of its practice, Ozick argues for a literature "not of the isolated lyrical imagination" but the liturgical communal speech that echoes the "voice of the Lord of History." Since American Jews define themselves as a religious community, they have the opportunity to yield not individuals like Moses Hess, Heine, Buber, Rosenzweig, or Baeck, but a culture and a literature. "Spain was for a time Jerusalem Displaced; psalms and songs came out of it. And Jerusalem Displaced is what we mean when we say Yavneh."[35] Joining in the effort to write the modern scriptures of the Jews, Ozick calls upon American Jewry to move forward with the task of creating another Jerusalem-in-exile.

Such an enterprise is only possible if a language Jewish in its concerns is ready for use, and Ozick claims that the American Jewish experience has prepared one. Its "New Yiddish" will be the language of multitudes of Jews, like "Old Yiddish" before Hitler; but as an American speech it will be liturgical and while not explicitly religious will help create a literature that will "passionately wallow in the human reality." The ambition underlying the effort is revolutionary, though, as some have noted, the anticipated tones and inflections are hard to imagine.[36] If Ozick is right, however, the result should be a culture and literature not of marginal human beings existing as outsiders, but of a profound examination of the condition of humanness from within a particular culture freed now of the tension of dual allegiances. Furthermore, the English of these writers would then become, like Aramaic, intertwined with Hebrew culture and tradition.

Ozick's program displaces the achievement of modern Jewish writing, in carrying forward the modernizing impulse of Yiddish culture, in favor of Hebrew and Zionist premises. It is not yet clear where such a program might lead. It does, however, suggest ways of comprehending the literary and cultural force of writers like Adele Wiseman, who charts the Canadian Jewish immigrant experience not just in terms of the outsider theme but the internal Hebraic dynamic and biblical memories of its inhabitants. In *Crackpot*, for example, the opening meditation on the cabalistic theme of the wholeness of vessels leads us into the tale of a young girl's coming of age and the ways in which she supports her blind father after her hunchback mother's death, by taking on the role of neighborhood prostitute.[37] It is an appropriate activity for a child conceived in the cemetery of a Polish town, in a public sexual spectacle staged by its superstitious peasants to halt the devastation of the plague. The naturalistic world of these characters provides them with a grim environment to deal with, and their satisfactions do not derive from increasing financial success and acceptance into non-Jewish society. The novel is a ladder of surprises, charting a psychology of imaginative responses resulting from a confrontation with terror. At its conclusion Hoda, prostitute become madam, meets a survivor of the Holocaust, aptly named Lazar, whom she marries. As he describes his escape from the bloody pit in which he had been left for dead by the Nazi firing squad, dragging himself through body, bone, and blood to a hiding place in the bushes and the succor of a peasant family, Hoda discovers an image matching her own effort to survive. The story has the Aggadic and enigmatic ring of a hasidic tale, like those of Rabbi Nahman of Bratslav. Human life, grim as well as joyous, finds here its liturgical celebration. *Crackpot* is permeated throughout by the ecstatic transformational power that *Call It Sleep* manages at its conclusion.

Ozick campaigns for "the Judaization of English, not only for the small community of Jews but for the wider world, so that Jewish writers may create their own literature and still hope to overcome the barriers of distinctiveness and particularism." Her fiction often has a midrashic quality. In commenting on the nature of things, her narrator often discovers that the web she sees in the outer world is the one in which she is implicated. "In drawing directly from Jewish sources" and Jewish culture, as Ruth Wisse observes, Ozick seeks to provide an "image of an alternative civilization." Her stories are "actually Jewish assaults on fields of Gentile influence."[38] If it is to be liturgical, such a literature must lead us back to a world where study of classical texts is a form of prayer, for both recreate their transcendental values for the Jews in everyday life. After the liberating energy of the modern break with tradition, in Yiddish as well as the other modern languages, it is appropriate to consider how the reinstituting of traditional values is possible. Whatever the achievement of the modern literatures and hyphenated Jewish cultures, Ozick, I suspect, believes them to possess only the momentary brilliance of the butterfly.[39] She would agree with Agnon's reported comment to Bellow: "Be sure you are translated into Hebrew, for only that lasts."

Like the Israeli writer, Ozick is committed to exploring the possibilities of sacredness in a world that denies them. She wonders if after the tradition and the Holocaust a Jewish life is possible. Ozick's remarkable story "Envy, or Yiddish in America" is an elegy to the destruction of Yiddish culture focused on the pettiness of its surviving writers in New York, who work impelled by the ghosts of their people and have no hope of issue without translation into English.[40] The story is wildly comic and deeply sad, chronicling the desperation of a poet seeking a way to exist in an alien tongue, as he searches for a young Jew who knows Yiddish well enough to comprehend its poetry and English so close to the bone to make translation possible. Encountering a young woman, Edelshtein, the poet and sterile husband, pursues her for this purpose of translation, a double-entendre central to the story. The result of his hopeless quest is to seal him in his envy of Ostropol, the successful Yiddish novelist well translated into English (modeled it is said on Bashevis Singer), and to leave us with an ironic sense of the degeneration of these remnants of a vital linguistic and cultural achievement now acting out the modern estrangement between their feelings and their words.

"Envy" is edged with a Jamesian irony, coupled with a biblical strangeness that evokes the power implicit in much contemporary Hebrew writing. Like the poetry, for example, of Dan Pagis, Ozick's writing elicits the biblical possibilities in contemporary life. (She captures the Yiddish rhythms of her characters in "Envy" but her narrator's words also have a greater formality to them.) If Ozick writes a book of lamentations and a Job story here, then Pagis invests the modern world with figures from the Bible much as Manger did. In one of Pagis' poems, Eve, the mother of us all, speaks from the sealed railway carriage en route to a death camp.

> here in this carload
> i am eve

> with abel my son
> if you see my other son
> cain son of man
> tell him that i

"Written in Pencil in the Sealed Railway-Car," the poem evokes an ancient myth and the first murder out of the experiences of the modern victims being transported to the death camps.[41]

Pagis stands at the point in modern Hebrew where he can marshal both classical and modern meanings in his words. Thus he parallels Agnon, who looked from classical texts toward contemporary Hebrew speech, while Ozick enacts the midrashic impulse in an English that might lead us back to a revitalized tradition. Pagis has more in common with Manger in their concern for the secular meanings of an absurd world. Ozick's call for a new Yiddish has a quixotic ring to it by contrast with the possibilities available to Pagis' modern Hebrew—still the language of the Bible as it is the spoken idiom of the modern Israeli. In reading his poem we are led to recognize that Jerusalem may yet be Zion, while New York may only by great feats of the imagination and perhaps sleight of hand become a modern Yavneh. The crucial issue here is the choice of language for the Jewish writer in a time when the possibilities for such choosing have become radically diminished.

We gain a further enlargement of this perspective in looking at a recent tale by another Israeli writer, Amos Oz. His story, published in *Commentary* as "Crusade" but originally entitled in Hebrew *Ad Movet*—literally and significantly "Unto Death" —recounts a typical incident in the long martyrology of Jewish history, especially its Christian, western European episode.[42] "Crusade" is the story of a band of knights led on a Jew-killing spree by their leader, Count Guillaume of Touron, on the way to the struggle with the Mohammedan infidel in the effort to recapture Palestine. Oz is aware of how that period of history was, for the Jews, a mini-genocide, almost a rehearsal for what nine centuries later Nazi culture, in this at least the heir of its Christian past, had in store for them.

By its nature, the mission of the knights turns out to be impossible; the knights end up turning upon themselves in order to root out the Jew in their own midst. First the poet is killed; then as the inquisition reaches in closer, they kill each other, until death for all remains the only possibility; the remaining survivors wander off into the forest in the middle of winter to encounter the meaninglessness of their lives. They have stripped their world of Jews and have thereby entered the void of nothingness. Böll's Hoysers—surrounded by wealth, wielders of authority—are discovered functioning in a similar realm by the Au. They grind on into a meaningless world where money and numbers have replaced personality. The Au. puzzles over their failure to ruin Leni just as he puzzled over the failure of the German bureaucracy of death to eradicate the memory of Boris.

Oz has told his story in a stark Hebrew. It is a remarkable feat of historical recreation by a Jew of a world dominated by non-Jews poised to destroy him. It is a realm in which a Jew speaks regally to preserve not his people's wealth or homes but their ancient books. Focusing on his heroism, Oz has pointed to the ways in which speaking is connected with storytelling, and both together form part of what we mean when we speak of tradition. He has done so in a language both ancient and modern and, in the process of coming to terms with the historical origins of the Holocaust, has helped to elaborate some of the possibilities of that old/new tongue.

Like Böll's, Oz's tale is an effort to map reality by exploring how to speak of the unspeakable—the defining events of our time which have confused the boundaries between reality and fiction, word and act. In the process, both tales force the reader to undergo linguistic versions of those hideous events, to experience the pain and suffering, in order to rediscover that biblical truth of the power of language through which the world was created. These tales of Sodom and Gomorrah are the negative moments of the dialectic that lead to more hopeful possibilities. Like Ozick, Böll and Oz write to comprehend how language rules even those who live in order to destroy it.

8
City Premises

The modern Jewish writer recapitulates the experience of a people moving from the shtetl into the ambiguous light of the modern city. As he recounts the tale of the marginal person in quest of the promised city, he confronts and articulates their intertwined, often inimical values and meanings. His account reveals the messianic desire to embrace the modern world, which propels Jewish character and people into modern history, and as well endows his writing with epic force. Examining the obstacles to Jewish acceptance, he elicits the ironies of the enterprise. As he portrays the ambivalent situation of the modern Jew, he is led to question, challenge, and revise the premises of his work: exploring the proffered conditions of citizenship, he reflects upon its purposes.

Much of my discussion entails things and contexts American and Jewish to emphasize the fact that, in discussing the modern world, one ought to pay attention to the limiting case. Reviewing some aspects of the process that led American society in the twentieth century to the frontiers of modernization, we are led to a question about the "end" of modern Jewish writing. With the writer we must consider the possibility that its purpose is assimilation into the mainstream. With the reader we must entertain the idea that its function is mythic, leading to identification with the process of the quest. Similarly, the confrontation of freethinker and conscious pariah produces two different yet related readings.

The freethinker claims that the purpose of modern Jewish writing is to bring about the assimilation of the Jew. For him, ethnicity is only a halfway house on the road to disappearance as an identifiable group. He sees little difference, for example, between Michael Gold's *Jews Without Money* and Henry Roth's *Call It Sleep:* both novels merely tell the story of immigrant hero and heroine leaving the narrow confines of the traditional order to reach for the openness and diversity of urban life. The interlinguistic function of Yiddish, so prominent in Roth's work and just as conspicuously absent from Gold's, is accounted for as stylistic accident. In this view there is a singular direction to modern Jewish writing. It conveys the dilemmas of individual and class mobility, like other ethnic writing, which it similarly helps to resolve.

The conscious pariah, by contrast, stresses the ways in which modern Jewish writing helps to redefine ethnic, religious, and national identity. For him the subtext of Yiddish is an informing structure; tradition is an abiding value in these works. For the freethinker, modern Jewish writing has a historical purpose in bringing the Jewish situation to a conclusion, whereas the conscious pariah claims that one kind of work has led to another, both recognizably Jewish in intent and purpose. For him the dimensions of this writing are multiple.

Just as Hawthorne and Melville explored religious and cultural issues to produce a literature examining the meaning of belief in a secularizing world, so the conscious pariah writes to analyze the conditions making for assimilation without necessarily embracing it as his own. The freethinker's interest in joining the mainstream leads him to ignore some of the historical and literary dimensions, just as the conservative Puritan or right-wing Jew relegates this writing to the modern or American experience, leaving "real" believers with the cultural agenda of tradition yet to be defined. In the case of the classic American writers as in that of the modern Jewish ones, a concern for the dialectical aspects of the cultural situation led them to create a many-sided writing.

These literary texts in the tradition of the conscious pariah— Henry Roth's by contrast with Michael Gold's—present the self as modern and traditional at the same time. They bring into the

center of the modern situation a set of values that revise it.
Therefore, Benya Krik, the hero of Babel's Odessa tales, is a triumphant rogue putting his modern violence and picaresque
talent for organization at the service of his Jewish community
and nation. My point of view depends upon an interlinguistic
reading of texts, in which interference is to be understood as
interreference. I will expand on it, but first let me indicate how
the freethinking view of Jewish, like the conservative Puritan,
reading of American history is reductionist. I will deal only
with the attack on Jewish history, leaving aside the response to
Puritanism.

The Jews of Western Europe entered the modern world as the
theories of civic, political, and religious reforms, propagated
during the Enlightenment, were culminating in the praxis of the
French Revolution. In 1791 the Assemblée Nationale recognized
Jews as citizens of the Republic, removing all legal restrictions
and granting them full equality.

With emancipation the status of the Jew, as it was defined in
medieval times and as it endured throughout the ancien régime,
changed. The secularization of society, the anticipation of the
victory of science and reason over religion and superstition,
undermined the old Christian conception of the Jew as wandering, degraded in his exile, until Christ's Second Coming. In the
past the social position of Jews had been based on religious differences, but religion itself was such a pervasive force that it
was able to structure an ethos that made this difference both
legitimate and ultimately meaningful. Merely to apprehend an
individual as, religiously, "a Jew" was sufficient to explain his
placement in terms ranging from cosmological to occupational.
By 1794, however, the cult of reason had become the religion of
the revolution. A fierce movement of "dechristianization"
(together with the spoiliation of churches and a massive transfer
of wealth) paradoxically produced a messianic proclamation:
"Religion is nothing but a mass of stupidities and absurdity . . .
A true republican cannot be superstitious; he bends the knee
before no idols; he worships liberty alone; he knows no other
cult than that of loving his country and its laws. The cross has

become, in the eyes of the humanist thinker, a counter-revolutionary emblem."[1]

The deterioration of religion as explanatory factor made the status of Jews an anomaly in both the logical and revolutionary senses. Emancipation changed the status of the Jew simply by making him a citizen and giving him equal rights. The problem, however, now became whether the rational and egalitarian heritage of the Enlightenment (and the radical antireligious fervor of the French Revolution) would prove to be as convincing an explanation for the new status of the Jew as medieval Christianity had proved to be for the older one. If it could, then antisemitism ought to disappear or at least be limited to reactionary individuals. But if antisemitism remained an institutional fact of European life, then its basis had to be sought in the failure of enlightened universalism to provide adequate answers. Finally, if it was not to be the recrudescence of the medieval Christian world view that accounted for the failure, then the rationale for the continued existence of institutionalized antisemitism had to lie elsewhere. In the next century, the emancipated Jewry of Western Europe moved out into Christian society to test these very hypotheses.

We are all aware of some of the forms that this testing took. There was, for example, Reform Judaism. Basing itself upon the Enlightenment, Reform attempted to modernize Judaism and make it consonant with the new age. Basing itself upon emancipation, Reform attempted to modernize Jews and thus make of them loyal citizens of the Mosaic faith. But rising European nationalism led to another rationale for antisemitism. As Rousseau gave way to Gobineau, there emerged a rationale for the status of the Jew potent enough to replace the supposedly discarded image of medieval Christianity. Henceforth the Jew could be excluded and despised for the most modern of reasons: raisons d'état. Zionism, the Jewish nationalism, responded in part to modern antisemitism by accepting its premises and demanding a country where the Jewish nation might develop its unique qualities. With socialism, from the ethical variety of Moses Hess to the most radical construals of Marx, the focus shifted from the emancipatory effects of the French Revolution, which was pronounced ultimately to be bourgeois, to the world-transforming effects of the socialist upheaval yet to come. Antisemitism was epiphenomenal to the class struggle, it was argued, and with the advent of the classless society, the Jewish problem, would disappear.

Amid the rise of these varied strategies for coping with the modern world, by changing, subverting, and revising some aspects of Jewish tradition (and reconstituting Jewish communal life to deal with the dynamic culture of the West), a new Jewish literature emerged. Parallel to other western literatures, it assumed the critical function of testing, proving, and trying out the strategies for modernization proposed by various groups or factions within the Jewish and non-Jewish world. In general, its purpose was to assess the impact of these varied strategies upon the individual and thereby articulate his relation to the communal group, at a time when the emergence of individualism as ethos and social actuality implied as well the dissolution of traditional communal ties. The content of this newly discovered Jewish individualism was problematic, making possible antitraditional freethinking and Zionist self-discovery, as well as the reconstitution of tradition and its subsequent focusing in wonder-working holy men or confused Sabbatean heretics. Writers claimed that their work might serve to explore and delineate ways of managing even that potentially schizophrenic lifestyle, of being a Jew at home and a citizen in the public realm so appealing to German Jewry. Thereby it could confront and help to temper the demands of the community in a time of crisis that threatened the hope of individualism and, with it, the very possibility of a modern literature.

It is important to note that the end of testing strategies for modernization implies methods not only for dealing with modernity but also for reconciling tradition. For example, even though Reform Judaism broke with tradition by relativizing it and seeing the law (*halacha*) of the community in historicist perspective, it nevertheless defined itself in relation to that revised tradition. Despite the claims of its critics, Reform Judaism did not promulgate a dialectic of the death of the old that would give birth to the new dispensation. In proposing a revision of Jewish tradition on the basis of a historically conceived reinterpretation, Abraham Geiger sought change rather than trans-valuation.

The translation of *Romeo and Juliet* into Yiddish that was used on Second Avenue changed Friar Laurence into a Reform rabbi. The resulting laughter of the delighted audience proved that in a play so obviously Jewish such a rabbi, confused about his relation to tradition, was still sufficiently within that heritage to function as the ritual agent of the lovers' union. In the wonderful expansiveness of Yiddish that saw any translation into the mother tongue as *farteicht und verbessert, Romeo and Juliet* became a Jewish play. The comedy of replacing friar with Reform rabbi came from recognizing that Reform Judaism had grasped the crucial horns of the dilemma of modern Judaism: How could a seemingly timeless tradition be revised? Part of the irony of the laughter must also have come from the realization that the beloved theater of the Yiddish masses could only be justified in terms of an acceptance of modernity. Purim had involved theatrical productions, probably since medieval times, but unless every day and season were carnival time, there could be no traditional justification for Yiddish drama.

The evident fact of the recent willingness of Reform Judaism to revise its earlier views, in particular of the importance of Zionism and the state of Israel, amounts to a proof of its place within the Jewish world. At the opposite pole, traditional Judaism crystallized into "orthodoxy" and thus also defined itself in relation to modernity, if only by varying degrees of rejection of it. But in contemporary America it is not orthodoxy that has thrived; nor has Reform become the single and united expression of "modern Judaism" as its founders anticipated. Instead it is Conservative Judaism that claims the largest numbers of Jewish-American adherents.

An American product, Conservative Judaism is a phenomenon of "third areas of settlement" and of third and succeeding generations. Unlike Reform it has not attempted to purge Judaism of its messianic character and, equally importantly, has developed to nurture the ethnic character of Jewish peoplehood. To invest in ethnicity is to validate the ties of blood, language, and kinship. It is above all an investment in tribal over civil ties. In a sense, then, the end of Judaism in America, with respect to tradition, has been recursive. If the American Jew truly feels that modernity is no longer problematic, so that he is indeed a full citizen of the West, then he ought to be content with classic Reform Judaism and accept his status as an American of the Mosaic persuasion. What we see, however, is that a significant number of people desire something more than a persuasional definition of self.

This brings us to the second usage of "end," as finish and conclusion. If by this is meant that soon there will be few Jewish writers who have experienced directly the dislocation of immigration and the *gemeinschaft* of the lower east side and its nurturing Yiddish—as there are fewer today who have experienced directly the culture of the shtetl—then surely we are coming to some sort of end, and there will be no more Bellows, Babels, and Henry Roths. It is clear, nevertheless that we have not in fact reached the end of the dialectical relation between free and critical thinker, and the impact of Yiddish on modern Jewish writing has not been concluded. In surveying its career, we do not observe a finished chapter in literary history punctuated, let us say, by the awarding of the Nobel Prize for Literature to Isaac Bashevis Singer. As Joyce Carol Oates notes, "Singer's engaging anecdotal style, the free-wheeling monologues of certain of Saul Bellow's characters, and even the grotesquely comic nightmare images of Kafka's fiction can surely be traced back to Sholom Aleichem."[2] Unless we accept the freethinker's utopian reductionism, the notion of "end" also has a double meaning.

The question is in part a political one. In America, as well as Europe, the freethinker has been in the vanguard of left-wing movements, and his abandonment of traditional culture has had a revolutionary purpose. Alfred Kazin captures the root meaning of the term in *A Walker in the City* in his description of his friend David, who left behind all his Jewish habits and bourgeois furniture, except for a set of Marx's works, and lived as close to the bone as possible in order to "think free."[3] In this image Kazin evokes the world of Gold's *Jews Without Money* —but unlike them the Jewish writer has been part of the mainstream of American culture in moving from leftist margins to the academic and professional center of the political spectrum and to relative economic security. Ironically, in Gold's powerful book, there is no interlinguistic activity. Though the story he tells focuses on the Yiddish-speaking Jews of the lower east side of New York, their entire experience is translated into English. True, he tells us at certain points that his characters are speaking Yiddish, but he does not dramatize that activity. As a result, his work lacks the linguistic and cultural riches of *Call It Sleep*.

Never in Gold's work does Yiddish interrupt the flow of the narrative to assert its claim as a cultural entity deserving of its own story. We gain more of a sense of Yiddish as language and culture from Hutchins Hapgood's *The Spirit of the Ghetto* than from *Jews Without Money* because the Anglo-Saxon writer has an anthropologist's curiosity about the linguistic crux of the situation he describes. Gold's linguistic reduction becomes a structural foreshortening; as everything is translated for the supposedly general audience he is addressing, differences recede. It is also worth noting that Isaac Rosenfeld's *Passage from Home*, remarkable as it is in other ways, shares some of these characteristics of Gold's work. Both novels address an audience universally conceived rather than one rooted in or concerned with urban ethnicity. This is perhaps less true for Rosenfeld than for Gold, who is intent upon the business of translating his city experience for a broad community of readers. Gold's protagonist never becomes anything so specific as a New York Jew, only a local participant-observer caught in the process of class transformation into a world citizen.

Communism, we know, was a particularly appealing strategy of modernization for the Jew. Ironically, and with few exceptions, as Daniel Aaron points out, the Jewish left-wing writer's "break with Communism became irreparable at that moment in American history when the barriers that had hemmed him in and kept him a 'hyphenate' began to crumble."[4] In "From Communism to *Commentary*," Aaron emphasizes the transformation of the Jewish freethinker's role in American life, and sees Jewish assimilation as incomplete. *Commentary* is a magazine of general opinion, yet recognizably and consistently Jewish in its major concerns. The former radical who writes for it has thereby reestablished his links to ancestral traditions even if only in an attenuated form. The point gets comic treatment in

Johanna Kaplan's *O My America*, where its central figure, radical writer and political activist Ez Slavin, takes as the moving principle of his life a quotation from the *Ethics of the Fathers:* "Love labor, hate lordship, and seek no intimacy with those in authority." Glimpsed framed over his desk by some of his students, it is promptly assumed to be a radical Chinese saying of ancient times.[5]

The complete assimilation of conventional wisdom is actually only partial. In America, "Jew" has become not a religious but an ethnic and even a national term. As such it has a different status and performs a different nurturing function for writer and people than traditional religious culture did, though they are closely related. Ethnicity has acquired a contemporary usefulness in testing modern values and providing strategies for coping with them. For the Jews, it has provided a partial disengagement from the modernization process and a distanced perspective on it.

Nevertheless, the power of ethnicity for securing Jewish identity in the modern world pales by comparison with the traditional way. This makes it peculiarly vulnerable to attacks from the right wing. Yet it is important to recognize that the notion of Jewish individualism is unthinkable without the mediation of ethnicity. In its absence, we have the communal force of corporate identity, perhaps best exemplified in the often ecstatic ritual gatherings and celebrations of the hasidic movement, surely a powerful response to the seductions of modernity even in its modernist rejection of them.

Isaac Rosenfeld defines the problem in *Passage from Home* when his protagonist meditates on his status: "For as a Jew, I was acquainted, as perhaps a Negro might be, with the alien and the divided aspect of life . . . I had come to know a certain homelessness in the world, and took it for granted as a part of nature; had seen in the family, and myself acquired, a sense of sadness from which both assurance and violence had forever vanished." Neither citizen nor corporate member, he hovers between. "We had accepted it unconsciously and without self-pity, as one might accept a sentence that had been passed generations ago, whose terms were still binding though its occasion had long been forgotten. The world is not entirely yours; and our reply is: very well then, not entirely." A Jew at home, a man outside—with personal gratification only to be found indoors. "There were moments, however, when this minor world was more than universe enough; times such as when grandfather would be raised to nobility, or when the family, gathered of a holiday, would distil so rare and joyful a spirit that all the assurance which had been lacking would rush back in flood, and one could feel the presence of God in it, and one could cry, 'This is reality, truth, beauty, freedom! What has the rest of the world to compare?' " To rely on the Jewish holidays as a separate and perhaps equal realm that for the moment allows these figures to realize their humanity and Jewishness at once is to deny one of the central habits of tradition, which constantly negated the notion that there might be another valuable world outside ritual ways. "But then, this too would vanish, and I would ask, 'What am I?' For as a Negro might ponder his outer body, asking himself why it should differ from other men's when inwardly he felt his common humanity, so I would consider my skin, my eyes, my hair, and wonder why I should feel an inner difference when outwardly I was the same as other men."[6] Neither home nor street is fully real, for in neither is he a complete human being. It is precisely that unclear non-Jewish world the protagonist crosses into when he leaves his family. He too will be an individual and autonomous person, something other than the embodiment of the heritage and values of his family and people. Nevertheless, the ambiguity of his status remains to plague him. If he feels his common humanity and unlike the Negro has no outward difference to mark him (despite the Nazi claim), still the inward difference remains.

The ambivalence of this passage structures Rosenfeld's novel: its pervasive elegiac sadness echoes the pathos of this sequence. At the end, the novel's youthful hero discovers that "our lives contain a secret, hidden from us. It is no more than the recognition of our failing; but to find it is all of courage, and to speak of it, the whole of truth."[7] Though he has ventured forth, his search reveals the failure of the possibility of significant individualism for him or the members of his family. The city here does not offer the possibility of ritual transformation that dominates *Call It Sleep*. Rosenfeld concludes only by sustaining the tone of sadness, an echo perhaps of Roth's conclusion yet lacking the ecstatic power that informs the latter. As a result, neither ethnic identification nor tradition is embraced, and only the abstract hope of common humanity remains, in a moment that echoes the conclusion of *Gatsby*, with Nick's sadness at being borne ceaselessly backwards by the current as he struggles against it.

Part of the elan of *Call It Sleep* derives from the religious force with which David Schearl pursues the immigrant's desire to find a place for himself. He struggles against spiritual and physical exile, the traditional explanation for Jewish homelessness. In his case, citizenship in the city of possibility is acquired at the cost of confrontation with the absolute power of the electric code that endows his city with a shape and form. Nevertheless, the novel concludes with David's muted summation: "One might as well call it sleep," which brings us back with him to the ambivalence of the resting place. We recognize that at best he has earned a respite from his struggle to achieve self-realization. Similarly, Rosenfeld's novel concludes at a moment of achieved self-consciousness, which points to the inadequacy of the freethinker's stance in both its failure and the discovery of its necessity. Tradition holds him back; family exerts its claim; and ethnicity remains in mid-path, looking both ways but perhaps leading to neither. Without the vibrant qualities of the Yiddish subtext of *Call It Sleep* to buoy up the possibilities of a modern revising of tradition that still retains its independence, *Passage from Home* charts the desperate need for the dream of citizenship at the same time that it demonstrates its impossibility.

In the work of Clive Sinclair, a young English Jewish writer with strong links to American culture, we find a sense of the openness, diversity, and possibility of the city.[8] In his work as in Kazin's we learn the pleasures of walking in the open air—a way of thinking and world making out of the multifaceted, nervy urban ambience. Sinclair, along with Grace Paley, parallels E. L. Doctorow's effort in *Ragtime* to present actual interethnic relations in the city. They pose the political issue: Who has the power to ensure the city's functioning as an arena that is home for all? At an ideological and literary level, this question becomes one of how to assure correct readings of a text—be it literary, linguistic, urban, ideological, or architectural—and thus ensure the sharing of assumptions by a diverse group.

Ragtime centers on the moment in American history when the city, with its mixed population of immigrants working together in a rough-and-tumble order, was about to be transformed by the mass ownership and use of the automobile. What was there in city life that made it possible for Jews, blacks, Irish, and the others to work together and yet made it so easy for them to break apart? In focusing his story on the interrelationships between Stanford White, Evelyn Nesbit, Father, Houdini, Mother, and the Baron Ashkenazy, as they participate in the tragic drama of Coalhouse Walker's life, Doctorow brings the history of the American city to bear on his tale. His account reveals how capitalism undermined the conditions that made urbanism possible in America, for its interest lay in promoting the marginal individualism of the car culture. In the novel, J. P. Morgan figures as the embodiment of the force of money in destroying the old possibilities, as he allies himself with the new technocratic class of inventors like Henry Ford. Together they invent the vehicular culture that takes us to the suburbs—a place where we can live with "our own kind"—in contrast to the city in which we live with all kinds.

Doctorow's inquiry focuses the historical problem. Given the stages of modernization brought about by dynamic capitalism, this seems an inevitable tactic to put the new immigrants and their explosive energy in its place, thus maintaining control through an order benefiting the new capitalism and its ruling class. It did offer suburbia, the private automobile, intense nuclear family interaction, and the management of conflict, with an ideal of family harmony, as a replacement for urbanism. The literary consequences of ghettoization in Levittown with modern appliances, one wife, and 2.3 children, like the social one, would imply the end of the possibility of citizenship, for Jew or black. The complexity of Doctorow's novel emerges when we realize that the Coalhouse Walker tragedy results from his desire to be an individual rather than a member of a class or ethnic group. As an artist, he knows the possibilities of individuality, for it is the condition of his achievement as composer and improviser of ragtime. As a human being, however, he believes that his wonderful car stamps him with a newfound freedom: this act is the beginning of his downfall. The Model-T Ford is also the vehicle that brings Houdini in contact with Father and

Mother, as all collide in the comedy of sputtering radiators and incomplete coitus with which the novel opens.

The figure of Houdini serves as the common focus for the city's multitudes and the upper classes, since everyone admires his skill and artistry. Nevertheless, like Coalhouse Walker, he too cannot escape from the role in which he has been imprisoned. For such an effort we need to link Houdini's artistry with the skill and subtlety of Freud. It is surely an oblique comment on Yiddish and the opportunity the language offers them for confronting the modern machine that brings Doctorow to link Freud and Houdini in calling them the "last of the great mother-lovers." The novel balances the grim shooting of Coalhouse (while the Morgan mansion is saved as the death-in-life museum of culture) with the optimistic story of the Baron Ashkenazy and his success in wooing Mother, culminating in the trek westward and the founding of a new industry. Hollywood and the American Dream center on the serial the Baron invents, *The Little Rascals*—a cinematic performance of the urbanism of city life and an enactment of brave possibility and ethnic cooperation. Thus, at the moment of the destruction of the American city at the hands of the tsars of cardom, the Jews founded a new industry—the movies. Creating the powerful genre of the city film that would have a world-wide impact, they celebrated an urban ideal.

One of the significant motifs in *Ragtime* is baseball. John McGraw and the New York Giants appear at key moments of the novel, to echo the movement of city life. Here Doctorow is seconded by Gunther Barth, who in his *City People* argues that baseball with its rules and rituals is central to the rise of urbanism in America.[9] Baseball and city life are experiences in surprise, rewarding alertness to new situations where split-second judgments depend on knowing how to take advantage of the breaks. Like walking in the city, which is a matter of feeling your way through space, so baseball is a game of the individual's constant negotiation with his changing environment. If football is a spectacle, made to order for television, its specialized actors reinforcing the mentality of suburbia with its emphasis on limited access, then baseball is a game of guidance through urban space and a set of rules for playing in its shared parameters.

Doctorow's novel blends fact and fancy, real and imagined figures, to conclude with a powerful image of the potential of art to chronicle the course of modern history and provide the possibility for a different outcome. In so doing, it manages to keep alive the values of a city culture by expressing the meanings in the idea of citizenship. Like Paley's and Sinclair's stories, *Ragtime* serves as a how-to book, presenting the ways one can function in the city and thereby devising a model of the territory in all its mysteriousness, difficulty, and possibility.

In focusing on social history, Doctorow brings together a wide array of characters and classes. The more intimate work of Sinclair and Paley takes the sweep of urban life as a backdrop and then focuses on the relation of intellectuals and power in the modern era. What Doctorow sets as his structural premise— the narrator's situation as city kid and urban thinker—becomes the problematic of Paley's and Sinclair's work. In their stories, the city protagonist tries to make sense of the urban world by moving through it in search of the object of desire, whether the hope of citizenship or the completion of passion. The sexual subtext of Doctorow's novel takes center stage in Paley and Sinclair, as they ask how the desired consummation identifies the protagonist and defines a character at once modern and ancient. For Paley, women and Yiddish culture keep company; for Sinclair, the marginal Yiddish Jew, the Los Angeles private eye, and the horrors of the Holocaust encounter a common destiny in the mysterious city of nightmare. In the work of both writers the desperation of contemporary city life receives appropriate chronicling. The result is a writing of revolutionary scope that, like Bellow's and Babel's, offers the possibility of liberation.

In focusing on the question of gender, and exploring the sexual encounters of men and women in the modern world, Paley highlights its revolutionary force. Her women are passionate. Their abandonment to desire becomes emblematic of the fate of all women as well as that of the Jews. Like Babel, Paley examines the consequences of world making through the liberation of this power. Her English is edged with Yiddish as is Babel's Russian, and both have a talent for using condensed images and filmic montage to propel the narrative to the moment of realization.

Sexuality as revolution forms Paley's recurring subject, with

the ways in which people (especially women) cope with the results (mostly children) its subsequent theme. Paley and Babel
see revolutionary energies as biological outpourings—the actual
subject of many of Paley's stories and an emergent one in Babel.
The consequences are intrinsic in the event, but no new worlds
are made. Though new human beings do not emerge from the
crucible of these revolutions, a reevaluation of those possessed
by revolutionary energies does occur, as well as a fuller assessment of the qualities of true revolutionaries. For women and
Jews make the revolution insofar as they remain faithful to their
identities, not as they embark upon ideological remaking in the
freethinking enterprise. Both writers use a similar narrative dialectic of concealment and revelation in order to avoid a psychological reductionism. The situations of these worlds are always
desperate, and redemption comes not with the Cossacks but in
the still small voice of reflection and consciousness. The mirror
of observation becomes the lamp of knowledge and understanding, illuminating with its steady light a fragmented world.

These stories are profoundly disturbing because they allow
us to see the sources and consequences of revolutionary passion. Babel and Paley reveal worlds whose social order cannot
deal with the passions except through political and sexual repression. In these realms, hero and heroine are forced into anar-
chism to escape the steamroller of social conformity, whether
imposed by suburban values or Bolshevik ideology. Paley's
women lead bohemian lives, just as Babel's protagonists evade
the demands of the commisar. The strategy they rely on is their
ability to accept confusion, chaos, and terror as givens of their
world and to maneuver through them by their wits. They are
citydwellers of the imagination, participants in the anarchic
ceremonial of urban life, which becomes for them ethos and
value. Their energy refreshes, and their thinking allows the
reader to consider the potential for redemption through democratic impudence and Jewish chutzpah. Paley's women are sexual democrats; Babel's men are revolutionary comrades. So
they situate themselves in the urban confusion and commit
themselves to the making of meaning within their worlds. They
focus on the here and now of their predicaments despite the allure of ideological seductions and metaphysical desire for un-
imaginable utopias.

From the perspective of the political left, these protagonists guarantee the failure of revolution. That is the desperation with which these characters live, on the edge of survival and madness, as the modern city they inhabit teeters on decay and sidles always toward final uninhabitability. They remain pariahs as the cities they love echo more and more their own inner states. The only possible redemption is through heightened consciousness—and the status of pariah is made bearable only by the act of becoming conscious of itself. Thus the stories of Babel, Paley, and Sinclair stress reflection upon their own state by their heroes, to the end that they may discover their own vocation, that of the conscious pariah. It may be that the political impact of these writings is negative, only teaching resistance to the modern world. But from the perspective of literature, they define an aesthetics of critical thinking and a perspective of simultaneous engagement and distancing that is central to the best in the modernist movement. The protagonist of our city myth knows that life is a gamble. The throw of the dice, however, is not only for advantage; chance and opportunity here depend as well on being able to stand up to modern times. If the heroes of these writings can confront the brute fact of power in their power-crazed century, country, and city, it is because they draw upon the resources of an ancient and powerful tradition.

Thus there is quiet hope at the end of *Call It Sleep*. And at the conclusion of *New York Jew:* "Across the river in Jersey a great fire is burning on the piers. The sky is maddened. From the party high over Lincoln Center, looking down on the plaza that from this distance looks more serene than it really is, in the midst of a rumble with a psychoanalyst about the 'neurotic guilt of survivors,' you can see the great fire raging, truly raging, on several Weehawken piers. Blaze was always my word for joy," Kazin notes. "Fire has haunted my life and I talk to my dead in my dreams—our dead—like those epic heroes who in the other world talked to their dead separated by a screen of fire. O Lord who made himself known as fire, where are you? . . . I want my God back. I will never give up until it is too late to expect you."[10] This is not the optimism of discovery of the form of the life and the myth, but the complex difficulty of moving between citizenship and subservience in the perhaps dying American city. The ambiguous endings of such works remind us that the reorientation of consciousness is not a rearrangement of power. For that, a political movement is needed, founded in cultural pluralism.

Does the current state of American Jews suggest the possibility of such a politics? Is such a view available in the intellectual subculture of America that is characterized by its freethinking? In Milton Gordon's words: "The general picture, then, appears to be one in which increasingly large numbers of Jewish intellectuals find themselves drawn by common intellectual and aesthetic interests and by professional activities and concerns into the buildup of the new, intellectual subsociety in America. They seem to find themselves sociologically and psychologically reasonably comfortable there, while a smaller number (which participates in the intellectual subsociety also) has, or searches for, more explicit ties to Jewish communal life and Jewish culture. In either case, the problems of marginality for the Jewish intellectual have clearly been considerably reduced."[11] With the abandonment of his hyphenate status in the sheltering confines of the American university, it may be expected that the Jewish intellectual will choose to end his Jewishness and step forward only as an American intellectual. It seems to me that we have witnessed the reemergence of the freethinker in our time but that, just as Jewish writers in the recent past found communism stifling, so too we can observe a younger generation turning from rationalism and ideological beliefs in order once more to make contact with ancient traditions. They are in the process of articulating a meaningful relation to tradition by beginning with an ethnic premise. Intellectual Jews no longer have to be freethinkers to prove their devotion to the academy; they have the option of critical thinking instead. They can make an eminently modern response and, instead of modernizing as their parents and grandparents did, engage in traditionalization. This is also a way of coping with the Holocaust as historical marker and modern phenomenon. The importance of Israel in contemporary American Jewish life has helped to elicit such a possibility, since its existence is in part predicated on a recursive notion of modernization. The political dimensions of its contemporary impact have also reinforced the need to face up to the variousness of Jewish experience in the modern world.

If the middle way of Conservative Judaism, here taken not just as an institutional movement but as an ethos, has become the definitive pattern of modern Judaism in America (and perhaps not only here), then we would expect to find a literature in which the communal group's deepest values, fears, and hopes are enacted by its representative individuals. The example of Sholom Aleichem therefore continues to be central, for his achievement lies in the way he articulated the meanings and values of the folk culture of Eastern European Jewry in his language as well as his fiction. In the choral commentator of his stories, he defined a modern listener to whom the oppressed and insulted Jews tell their life histories and, in making it possible for them to express their strongest as well as most typical experiences, he validates their individuality as ethnic participants in their community. Even the marginal intellectual and the Jewish writer reveal the roots of their literary achievement in a similar way, by charting an individuality profoundly implicated in the communal traditions from which it emerges. Portnoy's extravagances as well as Augie March's and Yakov Bok's journeys function in this way and, despite notable and tendentious misreadings, neither Portnoy's complaint nor Augie's adventures end up merely as roguish exploits. The irony of their actions are manifest in Portnoy's sexual impotence, when he encounters a sabra in Israel, and Augie's inability to cease his wanderings. The perspective of the cultural anthropologist, trained not to look to finite ends of cultural forms but to their evolution, is useful here. We need to consider other recent novels produced by Jewish Americans and see if they provide further evidence for cultural change rather than the conclusion of assimilation, though I shall not now attempt to convince you that *Fear of Flying* is a Jewish book. Instead, taking the notion of evolution seriously, I want to include some examples from a major twentieth-century American art form, the film.

One effect of the interlinguistic model is to increase our sensitivity to the many sources of a given language. It makes us aware of the ways in which some literary usages highlight word and phrase origins while others glide over them; and both instances can serve as indicators of the history of linguistic as well as cultural change. When lexical borrowings from contiguous languages and cultures become incorporated in a given tongue, the process of fusion is at work and may lead to the development of new languages and cultural configurations, which assert their independence in linguistic terms by "the rise of purely internal innovation."[12] An analogous process of cultural fusion operates when, for example, Harry Golden lists the English words that entered the Yiddish of New York's east side in the early twentieth century (in his commentary on Hutchins Hapgood) and thereby evokes a particular intercultural microcosm.[13] So does Woody Allen when in *Annie Hall* he juxtaposes his image as a modern suitor of Diane Keaton, eating dinner at her parents' midwestern home, with a vision of himself at the same table in full hasidic attire. In the movie Allen does not think of himself as an immigrant Jew but as an American; it is only when he sees himself through the eyes of Annie Hall's parents and grandmother that he realizes that as a Jew he is more of an intruder into their community than a prospective Christian son-in-law would be. His presence interferes with their cultural heritage, celebrated in the ritual of Sunday dinner. The interlinguistic model comes to a focus here in the concept of interference.

"Il faut lire l'intérfèrence comme inter-réfèrence," Michel Serres comments.[14] Woody Allen as Jew is an interruption of midwestern manners and the Protestant aesthetic of middle America because his presence so graphically refers back to his immigrant origins. Similarly, in the world of *Red Cavalry*, where Babel's narrator and his Cossack comrades are engaged in the messianic act of revolutionary transformation by breaking heads and spirits, Gedali interferes and thus functions as an interreference. His presence as a character, and his questioning of the values of the Revolution, forces the narrator to see his situation without ideological blinders. As a result, his characterization of Gedali's commitment to traditional Jewish culture translates it into the terms of modern culture in a phrase that reverberates ironically against the pretensions of the revolution. The story's concluding phrase—"Gedali, the founder of an Impossible International, has gone to the synagogue to pray"[15]— crossreferences the two realms and thereby reveals to the speaker, and with him the story's reader, the moral emptiness of a party that justifies wholesale murder by an analogy to breaking eggs for cooking an omelet. It is not the Revolution, the vanguard of modernity, that has created the International; rather, Jewish tradition has continued to assert and maintain its universal values by means of its concrete practices, even in the face of the self-deluding claims and power of modernization. As a result of Gedali's interference, the narrator and reader experience this moral irony in such a way as to make it impossible for either to continue as a freethinker.

An ironic effect is thus generated through the opposition between free and critical thinker. As we have seen, such a dialectic is a feature common to much of modern Jewish writing, and this function of plot is reinforced by parallels in style and tone. We see as well a common habit of drawing the reader into the story so as to make the irony come to rest in his own ambivalent situation. This often occurs by including the reader through the technique of direct address: he is the audience for and before whom the tale is told.[16] Sometimes this function is fulfilled by a commentator in the story who serves as the reader's surrogate. If the writer recapitulates the historical experience of his people, then the story as a whole is also one moment of that process. "Gedali," and tales like it, is an exemplar of critical thinking: it functions by evoking the traditional values behind the modern situation in allowing Yiddish, as language and culture, to make its presence felt in the character, situation, and narrative voice of the story, as it does in the vocabulary, syntax, and morphology of the western language in which it is written.

Babel, the critical thinker removed from traditional Jewish life, evokes a pluralist vision. Whatever its origins, like those of Yiddish, the full effect goes beyond linguistic and cultural sources and evokes not the apocalyptic messianism and eschatology of the communist revolution but the kernel of Jewish humanism at the center of Yiddish culture. Modern Jewish writing is thus a rewriting of the false promises of emancipation, modernization, and assimilation so that for the moment the Jew can be both modern human being and traditional Jew, thereby realizing the full dimensions of his humanity.

The structural situation of this writing—the interplay be-

tween free and critical thinker, the interlinguistic pressure of
language and style—is not so different from the situation of the
classic American writers. Despite their acceptance of nineteenth-
century stereotypes of Jews, they too reveal the pressure of a
traditional religious language in their work. They also chart the
interaction of atheist and believer and take a skeptical attitude
toward them even as—like the modern Jewish writer—they
manage a histrionic and at times ventriloquistic rendering of
both perspectives. And the classic American writer functions as
a critic of the modernizing strategies of American life as well as
an assessor of the continuing impact of its traditional values.

As Yiddish is the subtext for modern Jewish writing, so the
traditional language of American Puritanism is the subtext for
the classic American writer. The effect is interlinguistic and
interreferential. Characters who deny the validity of one realm
encounter its presence in the other, and the freethinker is baffled
by the continuing force of evil. His blindness to tradition pre-
vents him from recognizing the demands of family, folk, and
primordial relationships as he proceeds to honor only the modern secondary values and relationships. Like Young Goodman
Brown he becomes an ironic figure who, by the very terms of
his effort to understand, is foiled of full comprehension. Trying
like Ahab to reconstitute the bonds of traditional culture in
order to make them instrumental to his modern quest, he encounters the most elusive of enemies—himself. His search reveals his inability to find his true identity, for the language he
uses to conceive of reality is invaded by another set of terms
whose meanings and values he has attempted to obliterate, even
though they form the basis for his own partial understanding.
Thus, as Richard Poirier has argued, the achievement of the
classic American writers is to chart the linguistic ambiguity of
American culture in the process of articulating the complexity
of its fate.[17]

It is also worth noting that our interest in the classic American writer has to a large extent been fostered by Jewish literary
critics like Kazin. Self-consciously part of the modern movement, they rediscovered the dualities and ambivalences of the
classic American writer at the same time that they were exploring their own dual allegiance. By expressing the complexities of

the enterprise of American writing in its classic period, they made it possible for the achievement of the modern Jewish writer to be recognized. Studying one renaissance, these critics made it possible for another, closer to home, to emerge.

As if in response to the claim that modern Jewish writing is at an end, Philip Roth in *The Ghost Writer* charts the paradoxical ways in which the third generation, far removed from traditional Jewish culture, still assumes its forebears as literary fathers and, through a wild and incredible series of events, accepts the role of continuer of the tradition. In the recognition of the son, the father's values are validated, a pattern that evokes the conclusion of Babel's "Gedali."

In this brash novel, an older writer recalls his literary debut and engages us in the tribulations of his identity crisis. His encounter with an established writer whose work he has admired for some time leads him to an exploration of the meanings and purposes of art. The older Nathan Zuckerman, looking back at his youthful encounter with the distinguished writer E. I. Lonoff, attempts to sort out the results of his own writing, catalyzed by the events going on around him. What distinguishes this tale from other bildungsromans, in which we watch the hero coming into his own, is Roth's ability to present his protagonist's search for a literary tradition in which to place himself in terms of the discovery of his familial and tribal origins. We discover with him that the problems of a particular family are literary opportunities for the writer and his tradition.

The novel opens with the young Nathan Zuckerman, just twenty-three, with four newly minted stories to his credit, going off on a literary pilgrimage to the New England Berkshires to meet his favorite writer, Lonoff, and receive "patriarchal validation."[18] His literary father will have to substitute for his real father, with whom the young man is having difficulties because of the content of one of his stories. Young Zuckerman, a fictional version of the Philip Roth who wrote *Goodbye, Columbus,* has been writing sketches of family and friends so unflattering as to make his father consider him an antisemite.

Family relationships in this novel are intertwined with artistic ones. The book makes us wonder if anything is accomplished by unadorned truth-telling. Is that how to make your way in the world of publishing, so full of carping editors and critics, or should truth-telling be reserved for the intimacies of family and personal relationships? As might be expected, whenever someone begins to tell the truth in this novel, something bad soon happens, because Roth's satire allows us to see how sincere truth-telling is also part of the freethinker's pose. It is only when the imagination is brought into play that we can learn from experience, and this novel reveals the ways in which its protagonists finally allow their fantasy and imaginative worlds to change that experience.

Lonoff writes fantasy; Zuckerman writes, he tells us over and over, the truth. Nevertheless, both have escaped from the horrors of Jewish history and modern terror, Lonoff by fleeing with his parents from a Zhitomir pogrom, Zuckerman by staying within the narrow confines of his New Jersey life in a house with a finished basement. The snowstorm that rages outside Lonoff's house is part of the natural protection against the ravages of history, Zuckerman notes, that Lonoff has erected around himself. Those terrors are nevertheless present, for at the center of this novel about art and life is the problem of how to tell the truth about the Holocaust.

In the past, Lonoff befriended a young refugee woman; she was a student at the college where he teaches and is now trying to get him to donate his papers to Harvard, as well as to leave his New England wife and domicile and run away with her, Amy Bellette, to Florence. Zuckerman catches just a glimpse of Amy, and he too is ready to flee with her. Her head is much larger than her body, he observes, which seems to have been emaciated and worn down in her youth. Still she is fetching, and she speaks with just a trace of an accent. Roth reveals his genius as a novelist here, for Zuckerman imagines that this young woman is actually Anne Frank, who miraculously survived the death camps, found herself famous, and realized she could not reveal the fact of her survival to her father or the world once her diary had been published and dramatized. Her writing has changed her life. So, exchanging letters with Lonoff, she goes about creating a new existence and a new identity for herself, in an action parallel to that of the other characters in the novel, also writers and artists whose artistic abilities interfere with normal everyday expectations because they too bear witness to the extraordinary, even surreal potential of modern experience.

Zuckerman wonders what it would be like for him to marry Anne Frank and bring her home to meet his parents. Would that prove he was not an antisemite? Would it let them know that just like Anne Frank he too is only trying to record the variousness of Jewish experience in a world where history has forced the Jews into endless acts of self-protection? Her presence brings the Holocaust—perhaps the epitome of modern possibility—into the American landscape. She brings the possibilities and terrors of selfhood, individuality, and identity-making home to Zuckerman and Lonoff: we are back in Bashevis Singer's modern version of the biblical world of anguish and desperate possibility—one, we may see, not so far removed from Hawthorne's and Melville's.

In parallel fashion *The Ghost Writer* also raises a set of other questions: What, for example, does it mean for Jews to be writing candidly in English about their own experiences? In part, the result is a rush of patriotism and pride. Zuckerman compares his excitement on reading Lonoff's stories of "thwarted, secretive, imprisoned souls—a response to the same burden of exclusion and confinement that still weighed upon the lives of those who had raised me"—to his parents' pride at the establishment of the state of Israel in 1948. As Rachel Erteil notes, the collective task of modern Jewish writers has been to abolish external and internal stereotypes in order to allow them to articulate their own comprehension of the situation of the Jews.[19] Given his feelings of Jewish self-assertion and pride, can Nathan—and Philip Roth—truly be an antisemite? Or does his writing in all its unabashed and confessional detail signal the full entry of the Jews, warts and all, into American culture, as Israel's nationhood marks its entry into modern history?

One way in which this novel deals with these questions is by contrasting Nathan's and Lonoff's use of English. It is said of the older writer that his stories seem translated from the Yiddish. Lonoff's bearing, like that of his characters, bespeaks passivity, whereas Nathan's implies action and energy. In some ways they

are literary father and son. At the end of the novel Nathan is left
alone in Lonoff's house—everyone else has run off, propelled
by the explosions of their personal relationships—and Nathan
remains to ponder the events he has witnessed. "There's paper
on my desk," Lonoff tells him as he leaves in pursuit of his wife.
Write something, he says, sentencing his heir to explore the
complexities of family life in the twentieth century and Jewish
aspirations, just as he had been sentenced to discover the com-
plications of English.

Roth's style is fluid and supple, his English a nuanced blend
of innuendo, sarcasm, and irony. Like the action of his tale, it
links Roth not only to the classic American novelists but even
more closely to the Yiddish masters who preceded him and their
American Jewish avatars, of whom Lonoff is a typical example
in his echoes of Bernard Malamud, I. B. Singer, and even Saul
Bellow. It is an indication of that tradition that Roth's novel
takes place in New England, where Bellow's Herzog also becomes reconciled to his own personal and cultural history.
"Roth has followed the Jew into his new prosperity . . . with the
eye of the Yiddish writer filled with the experience of the Jewish
dilemma, regardless of the location."[20] In this way, Roth signals
the dual literary tradition in which he hopes to find his Jewish
place, reminding us as well that the work of his Yiddish forebears like his own and Bellow's is characterized not by polite-
ness and gentility but by vigor, panoramic sweep, irrepressible
wit, and style, as they attempt to make sense of the terrible col-
lision between modernity and tradition.

The breathtaking transitions of Roth's work, like the startling
juxtapositions of its extreme situations, is a characteristic shared
by Cynthia Ozick, Johanna Kaplan, Grace Paley, and Clive
Sinclair. Perhaps they are offering a literary parallel to the
revolutionary violence of modernity. This violence finds expression as well in contemporary Israeli fiction. Committed to
the modern world from its inception, Israel has provided its
writers with a host of national themes. In its classic fiction, the
ways in which traditional Jewish values are transformed into
modern Israeli habits, became a central motif, as in Agnon. For
the last two generations, Israeli writers have charted the tensions involved in becoming a Middle Eastern paragon of modernity. Ironically, they know that the triumph of their new sta-

tus has not produced world citizenship, and antizionism is today in many places nothing more than a code word for antisemitism. Writers like Amos Oz and A. B. Yehoshua pursue the inner ramifications and transformations of the dialectic struggle of modern Jewish history. Their work clarifies the dimensions of the revolutionary act of demanding not ethnic status but citizenship. Yakov Bok may imagine he will assassinate the tsar; Moses Herzog carries a gun; but only the Israeli writer understands that in order to become an agent of history rather than its object the modern Jew must have access like other modern nations and peoples to the machinery of violence. It is the lesson of the Warsaw ghetto uprising of 1943, counterpointed to the political helplessness of Eastern European Jews in the face of the Nazis. As Amos Oz likes to point out, the only thing Jewry in Poland lacked to make itself a nation—it had its own culture, language, and social institutions—was an army, and this missing element alone ensured its complete destruction.

Like the Israeli, the younger American Jewish writer does not focus on the dual allegiance of his characters. Instead, Jew and American share the same ambivalences in the modern world. Thus Houdini—a major figure in *Ragtime* and the focus of a recent work by Lynn Luria-Sukenick—is both at once. Who more American than Houdini the escape artist? Who more Jewish than the Houdini who appeared, the legend goes, in Dachau? "After this knowledge, Houdini," Sukenick asks, "what camouflage?"[21] As Jew and American artist, he is out in the open.

A similar theme is at work in *The Big Fix*, the recent film based on the 1973 novel by Roger Simon, starring Richard Dreyfuss. Here Dreyfuss plays Moses Wine: Jewish, a radical at Berkeley ten years before, now a private eye. Bulldog Drummond, Sam Spade, Philip Marlowe—but does a nice Jewish boy become a private eye? Yes, apparently he does, in America.

The night I saw *The Big Fix* it was playing next door to a film starring Burt Reynolds: the large, simple, engaging American boy, able to handle himself in bar or bed. Dreyfuss—the small, complex, annoying, ambivalent American boychik—portrayed something very different from Reynolds, but both theaters were full that night, for neither actor or projected image is less American than the other.

Esquire did a story on Dreyfuss, claiming him as a cultural symbol: his roles "capture the spirit of the urban intellectual caught up in the turmoil, energy and neurosis of that milieu. In his own way, Dreyfuss is a perfect reflection of life today in American cities."[22] Now it is important to note that in *The Big Fix* Dreyfuss explicitly plays a Jewish character. It is not his Jewishness, however, that is highlighted in *Esquire*'s remarks, but his identity as a modern, urban alienate.

In one scene in the film Dreyfuss confronts an antagonist. Both are searching for a former radical gone underground whose name is Sam Eppis ("Eppis" as in the Yiddish for "a little something"). And Dreyfuss complains, "Look, you're looking for Eppis, I'm looking for Eppis, the police are looking for Eppis —*everyone* is looking for Eppis!" Now what is the significance of Moses Wine, Jewish private eye, leading or symbolizing a general search for *eppis?*

The essential question that confronted the European Jew first leaving the ghetto had to do with identity: "Who am I? Who will I become? What will my children become?" There was a dizzying array of answers: "I am Reform; I am a Zionist; I am Marxist; I remain Orthodox." It is this question of identity— underscored by the dynamics of an immigrant experience—that has informed so much of modern Jewish writing.

But the progress of modernity has had a peculiar effect on the problem of identity: it has universalized it. Or, in America, we should say: it has democratized it. Everyone—Gentile and Jew —can now ask "Who am I?" and find their answers in new religions or new therapies—or old religions and old therapies. By the same stroke, the Jew has come to symbolize that modern problem. In the past it was commonly accepted that the Jew defined perfectly the sociological category of the marginal man, the pariah people; today many persons participate in modern progress and feel themselves similarly marginal.[23]

Perhaps, then, we have reached the "end of modern Jewish writing" only to begin the "Jewish writing of the modern situation." It will be Jewish at the same time that it is universal—or at least as universal as the modern, urban alienate himself. Richard Dreyfuss will not replace Burt Reynolds, but both may form two of the many images of late twentieth-century America. Far too often the Jew of the last two and a half centuries is portrayed as struggling against the engine of modern history and merely reacting passively to it. The inaccuracy of this image is evident, given the dazzling set of strategies he devised for grappling with it, which enabled him to cope with and transform it.

Encountering the modern world, the Jewish writer confronted a range of possibilities that led him to articulate his inquiry into the parameters of city life. The result was a body of writing that speaks for the idea of the city in a culture more and more intent upon abandoning it as an ideal just when the greater part of its population was being relegated to the urban condition. The tensions of this historical moment inform Johanna Kaplan's *O My America*, as she investigates the urban situation of the contemporary Jew in America.

What does it mean, the novel's protagonist Merry Slavin wonders, that her father Ezra came to America as a young boy and proceeded to construct a life for himself, ranging from freethinking to a concern for the fate of the Jews in the modern world? What led him to his critical writing, the stature of his stance as a social critic, the ease with which he moved from marriage to marriage, leaving behind an almost unknown, uncared-for progeny? As she embarks upon the effort to discover who he was, triggered perhaps by her thoughts about their coming dinner date, punctuated by the phone call that tells her of his heart attack and death, she discovers her own history.

This enterprise leads her to consider the meanings implicit in the myth we have been examining. The novel dramatizes the act of reading the story of the generation of Jews who escaped from their marginal and meager villages into the fabled metropolis of affluence and acceptance. In the process, Merry constructs the text of her father's life—or rather she invents and discovers the meanings of her father's life by assembling the narrative of her own prehistory. Following in her father's calling without his flamboyant idealism, she is the sober historian of their common destiny. In constructing a text out of a meditation on the meaning of her enigmatic, charismatic father, realistic, keen-eyed Merry plays Nick Carraway's role to another immigrant, Gatsby.

Like other classic American works, this novel proposes a

vision of America in process. It is a country constantly being invented by the actions of its inhabitants. The novel is highly self-conscious about its status as a story in a given time and place, whose central subject is similarly that of text-making. Almost all its major characters are writers, and Ez is the occasion for its existence as a novel. His life is the text his daughter is trying to write in the process of discovering her own situation. Thus the book celebrates the writing and making of America. Put another way, Merry seeks to clarify the possibilities after her father's death for her own liberation. The experience that led David Schearl in *Call It Sleep* to become a scapegoat, as he endeavored to become a New York Jew, is here echoed by Merry.

Her life is not only a city myth, she realizes, but the process of invention of the meanings of city life. What she discovers is that Ez is not only the first urban man of his American time, but that he offers her a way of learning how to continue to live in the city even as it decays. As Merry reflects upon the urban world in the course of her odyssey, she encounters some of its possibilities: "If I lived here . . . I would never be bored." For her too the city has become electric, a value in itself, rather than merely an environment for particular actions. Her father's stride becomes an embodiment of its meaning: "And even now, on dusky spring evenings, when she heard this cry, 'Take a giant step,' from children playing outside, five floors beneath her windows, it gave Merry back her earliest sense of Ez: Ez walking, musing and distant, with his broad, hopeful strides, nearly sliding up the block."[24] As a woman, Merry discovers her own life and her father's to be intertwined not only because her body bears his and her mother's genes, but because the city exists for her as their common matrix. Real as well as imagined, this city is the bodily shape they share. It is marked by Ez and his giant steps, as her body is marked by his being.

Merry projects this modern-day Thoreau and conscious Jewish pariah into the urban situation. He becomes its resident genius. Identifying with her father, Merry joins him in the statement of the novel's title, taken from "To His Mistress Going to Bed" in which John Donne describes his lover's body as the continent he wants to explore: "Licence my roaving hands, and let them go, / Before, behind, between, above, below, / O my America, my new-found-land, / My kingdome." In constructing the text of Ez's life, Merry participates with him in the seducing act of the modern imagination, creating for us the city in which she exists, Ez's kingdom. He has brought her to it like a modern version of his biblical namesake, who taught the Jews to read their sacred text as he showed them the importance of rebuilding their ancient urban capital. Ezra Slavin thereby teaches his daughter how to be freed from the bondage of the past while bringing into the heart of modern life the values of tradition.

Merry's last realization in the book echoes the first. She imagines Ez looking at a racing form left on the table of a cafeteria. The image reveals the full extent of her relationship: father and daughter, like the city they live in, are gamblers. Not just any city, to be sure, but the American city: New York, which Ez had always loved because it was always changing. Democratic, dynamic, and open, New York offers them the possibility of articulating its values by participating in its life as citizens and makers. Embracing the urban condition, these characters take their identity from the city premises they help to shape and celebrate.

Notes

1. An Urban Phenomenon

1. Robert E. Park, "Human Migration and the Marginal Man," in *Classic Essays on the Culture of Cities*, ed. Richard Sennett (New York: Appleton-Century-Crofts, 1969), p. 141.

2. Alfred Kazin, *New York Jew* (New York: Knopf, 1978), p. 3.

3. Ibid., pp. 3-4.

4. Henry Roth, *Call It Sleep* (New York: Robert O. Ballou, 1934), p. 37.

5. Louis Wirth, "Urbanism as a Way of Life," *Classic Essays on the Culture of Cities*, p. 156.

6. Also see Bonnie Lyons, *Henry Roth: The Man and His Work* (New York: Cooper Square Publishers, 1976), pp. 111, 118.

7. Kazin, *New York Jew*, pp. 288, 295.

8. Alfred Kazin, *A Walker in the City* (New York: Harcourt, Brace, and World, 1951), p. 1.

9. Hannah Arendt, "The Jew as Pariah: A Hidden Tradition," *The Jew as Pariah: Jewish Identity and Politics in the Modern Age*, ed. Ron H. Feldman (New York: Grove Press, 1978), p. 83.

10. Louis Simpson, "Baruch," *Searching for the Ox* (New York: Morrow, 1976), p. 62.

2. Dual Allegiances

1. See Donald Fanger, *Dostoevsky and Romantic Realism: A Study of Dostoevsky in Relation to Balzac, Dickens, and Gogol* (Cambridge: Harvard University Press, 1965); Michael Cowan, "Walkers in the Street: American Writers and the Modern City," *Prospects*, Fall 1981.

2. The absurd but accurate logic of this situation drove Isaac Deutscher, for example, to call himself a non-Jewish Jew. See his *The Non-Jewish Jew and Other Essays*, ed. Tamara Deutscher (London: Oxford University Press, 1968).

3. *A Bintel Brief*, ed. Isaac Metzker, trans. Diana Shalet Levy (New York: Doubleday, 1971), pp. 97-99.

4. See Abraham Cahan, *The Rise of David Levinsky* (New York: Harper, 1960); Alfred Kazin, *A Walker in the City* (New York: Harcourt, Brace, 1951), p. 60.

5. Allen Guttmann, *The Jewish Writer in America* (New York: Oxford University Press, 1971), p. 12.

6. Hannah Arendt, *The Jew as Pariah: Jewish Identity and Politics in the Modern Age*, ed. Ron H. Feldman (New York: Grove Press, 1978), pp. 18, 67-68.

7. Thorstein Veblen, "The Intellectual Pre-Eminence of Jews in Modern Europe," *Essays in Our Changing Order*, ed. Leon Ardzrooni (New York: Viking, 1954), pp. 229-230, quoted by Guttmann, *Jewish Writer*, p. 136.

8. Robert E. Park, "Human Migration and the Marginal Man," quoted by Guttmann, *Jewish Writer*, p. 134.

9. Arendt, *Jew as Pariah*, p. 134.

10. Veblen, "Intellectual Pre-Eminence," *Essays in Our Changing Order*, pp. 229-230.

11. Arendt, *Jew as Pariah*, p. 68. Also see Max Horkheimer and Theodor W. Adorno, *Dialectic of Enlightenment*, trans. John Cumming (New York: Herder and Herder, 1972).

12. Richard Stern, *The Books in Fred Hampton's Apartment* (New York: Dutton, 1973), p. 153.

13. Ibid., pp. 154-155.

14. "I am writing of things long forgotten": dedication to *You Must Know Everything*, trans. Max Hayward, ed. Nathalie Babel (New York: Farrar, Straus, and Giroux, 1969), p. 1.

15. The phrase is Robert Alter's and serves also as the title of his book (New York: Jewish Publication Society, 1977).

16. See Philip Roth's "Eli the Fanatic" in *Goodbye, Columbus* (New York: Houghton Mifflin, 1959).

17. Hannah Arendt, *The Human Condition* (Chicago: University of Chicago Press, 1958), p. 166.

18. Bernard Malamud, "The Jewbird," in *Idiots First* (New York: Farrar, Straus, 1964), pp. 101, 102, 112.

19. See John M. Ellis, *The Theory of Literary Criticism: A Logical Analysis* (Berkeley: University of California Press, 1974), esp. chaps. 5 and 8; David Neal Miller, "Fear of Fiction: Narrative Strategies in

the Works of Sh. Rabinovitsh (Sholom Aleykhem) and Isaac Bashevis Singer" (diss., University of California, Santa Cruz, 1981).

20. Michael Halliday, *Language as Social Semiotic* (London: Arnold, 1978,), p. 4.

21. See the essays by Dell Hymes, James Fox, and Barbara Kirshenblatt-Gimblett in *Explorations in the Ethnography of Speaking*, ed. Richard Bauman and Joel Sherzer (Cambridge, Eng.: Cambridge University Press, 1974).

22. I. B. Singer, "The Spinoza of Market Street," in *The Spinoza of Market Street*, trans. Martha Glicklich (New York: Farrar, Straus, and Cudahy, 1961), p. 23. The Yiddish original is Yitzhok Bashevis |-Zinger], "Der spinozist," in *Gimpl tam un andere dertseylungen* (New York: Tsiko, 1963), p. 32.

23. See James A. Matisoff, *Blessings, Curses, Hopes and Fears: Psycho-Ostensive Expressions in Yiddish* (Philadelphia: Institute for the Study of Human Issues, 1979).

24. Walter Benjamin, "The Task of the Translator," in *Illuminations*, ed. Hannah Arendt, trans. Harry Zohn (New York: Harcourt, Brace and World, 1968), pp. 79, 82.

25. Philip Roth, *The Ghost Writer* (Farrar, Straus, and Giroux, 1979), p. 27.

26. Saul Bellow, *Great Jewish Short Stories*, (New York: Dell-Laurel, 1963), p. 16.

27. Isaac Babel, "Gedali," *Collected Stories*, trans. Walter Morison, introduction by Lionel Trilling (New York: Meridian, 1960), p. 72. Chone Shmeruk commented in a conversation we had at the Oxford Conference on Research in Yiddish Language and Literature, August 1979, that Babel plays Russian against Yiddish most self-consciously in these stories. Also see Efraim Sicher, "Isaac Babel's Jewish Roots," *Jewish Quarterly*, 25 (Autumn 1977), 25-27, as well as Sicher's recently completed dissertation on this subject for the Russian and Slavics Department, Wolfson College, Oxford.

28. "Awakening," *Collected Stories*, p. 313. Morison translates: " 'My child,' she said to him in Hebrew, 'our grief is great. It has no bounds. Only blood was lacking in our house. I do not wish to see blood in our house.' " It is clear that they were speaking Yiddish.

3. Clothing and Character

1. Richard Stern, *The Books in Fred Hampton's Apartment* (New York: Dutton, 1973), pp. 148-149, 244, 247.

2. Henry Roth, *Call It Sleep* (New York: Robert O. Ballou, 1935), pp. 3-4.

3. Ibid., pp. 11-12.

4. Richard J. Fein, "The Rise of David Levinsky and the Migrant Self," *Studies in American Jewish Literature*, 2 (Spring 1976), p. 2.

5. Bellow's introduction to *Great Jewish Short Stories*, ed. Saul Bellow (New York: Dell-Laurel, 1963), p. 10.

6. Philip Roth, "Eli the Fanatic," *Goodbye, Columbus and Five Short Stories* (Boston: Houghton Mifflin, 1959), p. 298.

7. Ibid., p. 297.

8. See notes 5 and 6 to Chapter 5 for some key readings. Thomas R. Edwards, "People in Trouble," *New York Review of Books*, 20 July 1972, p. 22, quoted by Ben Siegel in "The Jew as Underground/Confidence Man: I. B. Singer's *Enemies, a Love Story*," *Studies in the Novel*, 10 (Winter 1978), 404.

9. "The Bus," *The New Yorker*, 28 August 1978, p. 33.

10. *A Treasury of Yiddish Stories*, ed. Irving Howe and Eliezer Greenberg (New York: Schocken, 1973), pp. 116-117.

11. Ibid., p. 118.

12. Ibid., p. 539.

13. Ibid., p. 540.

14. Ibid., p. 531; the shoe advertisement is on p. 541.

15. Singer also uses the Hebrew *Baal-mesacha* for the craft. The key use of *arbeit* comes at the end of the story. *Gimpel the Fool and Other Stories* (New York: Central Yiddish Culture Organization, 1963), p. 42.

16. Howe and Greenberg, *A Treasury of Yiddish Stories*, pp. 526-527.

17. Ibid., pp. 543-544.

18. *Enemies, a Love Story* (New York: Farrar, Straus, and Giroux, 1972), p. 15.

19. Ibid., p. 62.

20. Ibid., p. 230.

4. Abishag: The Body's Song

1. Hannah Arendt, *The Human Condition* (Chicago: University of Chicago Press, 1958), p. 166.

2. *An Anthology of Modern Yiddish Poetry* (New York: October House, 1966), pp. 20-23. Manger's Abishag cycle is in the *Lied un Balade* (New York: Itzik-Manger-Comitet, 1952), pp. 254-261. Except where otherwise noted, translations are my own. The four poems are: "Abishag," "Abishag's Last Night in the Village," "King David and Abishag," and "Abishag Writes a Letter Home."

3. Babylonian Talmud, Tractate Sanhedrin 22a, 39b. Also see the entry in *Encyclopedia Judaica*.

4. Jacob Glatstein, "Abishag," *Fun Mayn Gantser mi* (Of All My Labor; Collected Poems, 1919-1956; New York, 1956), p. 360, originally published in *Fraye Ferzn* (New York: Groyer Stodolski, 1926). I have referred to the translation in *The Golden Peacock*, ed. Joseph Leftwich (London: Ashcombe, 1939), pp. 333-334.

5. Gladys Schmitt, *David, the King* (New York: Dial, 1946; reissued 1973). For Rilke's poems I have referred to Rainer Maria Rilke, *New Poems*, trans. J. B. Leishman (New York: New Directions, 1964). "Abisag" is in the First Part, p. 58.

6. See Brian Murdock, "A Yiddish Writer and the German Cultural Hegemony Before World War II," *Jewish Social Studies* (April 1973), 103-104.

7. Franz Rosenzweig, *The Star of Redemption*, trans. from the 2nd ed. of 1930 by William W. Hallo (London: Routledge and Kegan Paul, 1970), pp. 77-79.

8. Ibid., p. 77.

9. Ibid., p. 209. The expressive "drag of the ground" I owe to Harold Fisch, who also called my attention to Rosenzweig.

10. Schmitt, p. 599.

11. Ibid., p. 600.

12. Ibid., p. 621.

5. Community and Modernity: Sholom Aleichem

1. "Geese," *Stories and Satires by Sholom Aleichem*, trans. Sholom Aleichem (New York: T. Yoseloff, 1959), pp. 116-117.

2. "Three Widows," ibid., p. 182.

3. Ibid., p. 183.

4. Both Gogol and Mark Twain use a similar strategy (with significant differences), prompting comparisons with Sholom Aleichem. On some similar Gogolian techniques see my essay, "Gogol's *The Overcoat* as a Picaresque Epic," *Dalhousie Review*, 46 (Summer 1966), 186-199.

5. Guillén, "The Anatomies of Roguery" (diss., Harvard University, 1953), p. 383, quoted by Robert Alter, *Rogue's Progress: Studies in the Picaresque Novel* (Cambridge: Harvard University Press, 1964), p. 3. Also see Howard Mancing, "The Deceptiveness of *Lazarillo de Tormes*," *PMLA*, 90 (May 1975), 426-432, who makes an argument like mine.

6. Joseph Silverman, "Sobre el arte de no renunciar a nada," *Papeles de los Armadans*, 221-222 (August-September 1974), 129-142, which also serves as the introduction to *Bibliografià razonada y anotada de las obras maestras de la novela picaresca espanola de Joseph V.*

Ricapito (Madrid: Editorial Castalia, 1975). Silverman's work on the picaresque is of crucial significance for understanding the role of the *converso* in the emergence of the genre. Among others see his essay, "Some Aspects of Literature and Life in the Golden Age of Spain," *Estudios de Literatura española ofrecidos a Marcos A. Morínigo* (Madrid, 1971), pp. 133-170. Also see Ulrich Wicks, "The Nature of Picaresque Narrative: A Modal Approach," *PMLA*, 89 (March 1974), 240-249.

7. See Ruth R. Wisse, *The Schlemiel as Modern Hero* (Chicago: University of Chicago Press, 1971), pp. 46-47, 53.

8. Ibid., pp. 44, 12.

9. *A Treasury of Yiddish Stories*, ed. Irving Howe and Eliezer Greenberg (New York: Schocken, 1973), p. 610.

10. "Geese," *Stories and Satires*, p. 124.

11. Ibid., p. 125.

12. Ibid.

13. Ibid., pp. 126-127.

14. Irving Howe, "Sholom Aleichem: Voice of Our Past," *A World More Attractive* (New York: Horizon, 1963), pp. 208-209.

15. Wisse, pp. 54-55.

16. "Happy New Year," *Stories and Satires*, pp. 160-165.

17. Ibid., pp. 167-169.

18. Jacob Katz, *Tradition and Crisis: Jewish Society at the End of the Middle Ages* (New York: Schocken, 1971), pp. 206-207.

19. "Three Widows," *Stories and Satires*, p. 184.

20. Ibid., p. 209.

21. Ibid., p. 212.

22. Ibid., p. 195.

23. Ibid., p. 201.

24. Ibid., p. 213.

25. Ramón Pérez de Ayala, *Belarmino and Apolonio*, trans. Murray Baumgarten and Gabriel Berns (Berkeley: University of California Press, 1971), p. 189.

6. Folk Speech and Holy Tongue: Agnon and Borges

1. S. Y. Agnon, "The Scribe," in *Twenty One Stories*, ed. N. Glatzer (New York: Schocken, 1970), p. 18. The story is translated by I. Franck from the Hebrew of "Agadat Hasofer," in *Elu veElu*, vol. 2 of *Kol Sipurav shel S. Y. Agnon* (Collected Tales; Jerusalem and Tel Aviv: Schocken, 1959), p. 139.

2. Jorge Luis Borges, "Averroes' Search," in *Labyrinths*, ed. by Donald Yates and James Irby (New York: New Directions, 1962), p.

148. The story is translated by James Irby from the Spanish, "La Busca de Averroes," in *El Aleph* of the *Obras completas* (Buenos Aires: Emecé Editores, 1967), pp. 91-92.

3. "An Autobiographical Essay," *Aleph and Other Stories, 1933-1969*, trans. Norman Thomas Di Giovanni (New York: Dutton, 1971), p. 137.

4. The phrase and the idea are central to E. H. Gombrich's *Art and Illusion* (New York: Pantheon, 1960), and particularly well developed in his essay, "The Mask and the Face," *Art, Perception and Reality* (Baltimore: Johns Hopkins University Press, 1970), esp. pp. 17, 35, 44-45.

5. It appears as vol. 7 of *Kol Sipurav;* the English translation from which I quote is by Walter Lever, *Two Tales by S. Y. Agnon: "Betrothed" and "Edo and Enam"* (New York: Schocken, 1966).

6. "The Garden of Forking Paths," *Labyrinths*, pp. 24-26, trans. Donald Yates from the Spanish, "El Jardín de senderos que se bifurcan," in *Ficciones*, pp. 104-107.

7. See Harold Fisch, "The Dreaming Narrator in S. Y. Agnon," *Novel*, 4 (1970), 68-69; the material has been incorporated in his *S. Y. Agnon* (New York: Ungar, 1975).

8. Jaime Alazraki, "Borges and the Kabbalah," *Triquarterly*, 25 (1972), 248.

9. See Gershom Scholem, "Reflections on S. Y. Agnon," *Commentary* 44:6 (December 1967), esp. 59-60; Jaime Alazraki, "Borges, or Style as an Invisible Worker," *Style*, 9:3 (Summer 1975), 325, and his "Borges and the Kabbalah," pp. 266-267.

10. Baruch Hochman, *The Fiction of S. Y. Agnon* (Ithaca and London: Cornell University Press, 1970), p. 25; Arnold Band, *Nostalgia and Nightmare: A Study in the Fiction of S. Y. Agnon* (Berkeley and Los Angeles: University of California Press, 1968), p. 49. For a theoretical discussion of the relations between Yiddish and Hebrew, see Itamar Even-Zohar, "Polysystem Theory," *Poetics Today*, 1:1-2 (1979), 287-310, and his "Aspects of the Hebrew-Yiddish Polysystem," a paper presented to the International Conference on Research in Yiddish Language and Literature, Oxford Centre for Postgraduate Hebrew Studies (Oxford, August 1979).

11. Band, p. 394.

12. Ruth R. Wisse, *The Schlemiel as Modern Hero* (Chicago: Chicago University Press, 1971), pp. 46-47.

13. Edward Alexander, *The Resonance of Dust* (Columbus: Ohio State University Press, 1979), p. 168.

14. I. B. Singer, *Enemies, a Love Story* (New York: Farrar, Straus,

and Giroux, 1972), p. 172.

15. John Bayley, "Character and Consciousness," *New Literary History*, 2 (Winter 1974), 225-227; Maurice Natanson, "Solipsism and Sociality," ibid., p. 243.

16. "Preface" to *Doctor Brodie's Report*, trans. Norman Thomas Di Giovanni in collaboration with Borges (New York: Dutton, 1972), p. 11, quoted by Alazraki in "Borges, or Style as an Invisible Worker," n. 28.

17. See Scholem, "Reflections," p. 59, and Alazraki, "Borges and the Kabbalah," p. 248, 266-267.

18. Band, p. 387.

19. Agnon's story appears in English in *Twenty One Stories*, pp. 162-168, trans. Misha Louvish; Borges' is in *Labyrinths*, pp. 76-87, trans. Donald Yates.

20. *Twenty One Stories*, p. 162, "Hapanim Lepanim," from *Samukh Venireh*, vol. 6 of *Kol Sipurav*, p. 205.

21. Ibid., p. 162; Hebrew, p. 205.

22. Ibid., pp. 163-165; Hebrew, pp. 205-208.

23. Ibid., p. 168; Hebrew, p. 210.

24. See Band's comment, in *Nostalgia and Nightmare*, p. 332. It is worth noting that in the title and theme of the story at least three biblical passages, Genesis 31:31, 33:20, and Exodus 33:11, are alluded to, all on the theme of seeing God face to face.

25. *Labyrinths*, p. 76; "La Muerte y La Brújula," in *Ficciones*, pp. 143-144.

26. *Labyrinths*, p. 77; Spanish, pp. 144-145.

27. Ibid., p. 78; Spanish, pp. 144-145.

7. Language Rules

1. The fullest study is Alvin H. Rosenfeld, *A Double Dying: Reflections on Holocaust Literature* (Bloomington: Indiana University Press, 1980), esp. "Poetics of Expiration," pp. 82-95.

2. George Steiner's is the classic work. See "The Hollow Miracle," *Language and Silence* (New York: Atheneum, 1967).

3. Rosenfeld, pp. 131-138.

4. Heinrich Böll, *Group Portrait with Lady*, trans. Leila Vennewitz (New York: McGraw-Hill, 1973), p. 78.

5. Ibid., pp. 90-91.

6. Ibid., p. 328.

7. Ibid., p. 360.

8. Hannah Arendt, *Eichmann in Jerusalem: A Report on the Banality of Evil* (New York: Viking, 1963).

9. "The subject of the Holocaust is explicitly introduced into *Mr.*

Sammler's Planet by means of a ferocious attack by the novel's protagonist on Hannah Arendt's thesis that Eichmann was the most ordinary of men, virtually a cliche, and that in general, the perpetrators of the unspeakable evil of the death camps were not great criminals but just the petty bureaucrats everywhere produced by the principle of division of labor." Edward Alexander, "Imagining the Holocaust: *Mr. Sammler's Planet*, and Others," *Judaism*, 22 (Summer 1973), 288.

10. Arendt, pp. 230-231.

11. Sol Gittleman, *From Shtetl to Suburbia* (Boston: Beacon Press, 1978), p. 120.

12. Arendt, p. 80.

13. Ibid., p. 81.

14. Ibid., pp. 81-82.

15. Böll, pp. 341-342, 346-347.

16. Arendt, p. 43.

17. J. S. Mill, *Autobiography and Literary Essays*, ed. J. M. Robson and J. Stillinger (Toronto: University of Toronto Press, 1981), pp. 245-246.

18. "The Ten Martyrs," selected from the Talmud and Midrash, in *A Jewish Reader*, ed. Nahum N. Glatzer (New York: Schocken, 1946), p. 183. In Chaim Raphael's translation, the entire passage is: "His daughter called out: O Father: that I should see you in this state! He replied: If I alone were being burned, it would have been a hard thing to bear; but now that I am being burned with the Scroll, He who will have regard for the plight of the Torah will also have regard for my plight. His disciples called out: Rabbi, what do you see? He answered: The parchment is burning, but the letters are soaring out on high." Chaim Raphael, *The Walls of Jerusalem: An Excursion into Jewish History* (New York: Knopf, 1968), p. 194, quoted from the Talmud, Abodah Zarah 17-18a. The rabbis recognized the impact of this story when they made it part of the Midrash Asarah Harugei Malkhuth—the account of the Ten Martyrs at the hands of the Romans—and made it a Selihah (penitential prayer) and an important part of the Yom Kippur and Tisha B'Av services. The rabbis' response to the crisis caused by the destruction of the Temple—by the Babylonians and the Romans—is explored in Raphael's valuable study, which sheds much light on Jewish modes of dealing with historical catastrophes approaching the order and magnitude of the Holocaust. Confronting the historical cataclysm of the end of Jewish statehood and independence in the first and second centuries of the common era, the rabbis found a way to continue the tradition. Their secret is to interpret it—to make of it a midrash (an exegetical retelling)—as if to prefigure Isak Dinesen's famous comment about storytelling.

19. André Schwarz-Bart, *The Last of the Just* (New York: Atheneum, 1961), p. 368.

20. Felix Weltsch, "The Rise and Fall of the Jewish-German Symbiosis: The Case of Franz Kafka," *The World of Franz Kafka*, ed. J. P. Stern (New York: Holt, Rinehart and Winston, 1980), p. 48.

21. Joyce Crick, "Kafka and the Muirs," *The World of Franz Kafka*, p. 164.

22. Simon B. Herman, "Explorations in the Social Psychology of Language," *Readings in the Sociology of Language*, ed. Joshua A. Fishman (The Hague: Mouton, 1968), pp. 500, 508.

23. Crick, p. 164; Wolfgang Fischer, "Kafka Without a World," *The World of Franz Kafka*, p. 225.

24. Chaim Weizmann, *Trial and Error* (New York: Harper, 1949), p. 53. Franz Kafka, "An Introductory Talk on the Yiddish Language," *Wedding Preparations in the Country and other Posthumous Prose Writings*, trans. Ernst Kaiser and Eithne Wilkins (London: Secker and Warburg, 1954), p. 418. The German original is in *Hochzeitsvorbereitungen auf dem Lande und andere Prosa aus dem Nachlass* (New York: Schocken, 1966), pp. 421-426.

25. Rosemary Dinnage, "Under the Harrow," *The World of Franz Kafka*, p. 75.

26. Kafka, "An Introductory Talk on the Yiddish Language," pp. 418-419, 420, 422.

27. Hutchins Hapgood, *The Spirit of the Ghetto* (New York: Funk and Wagnalls, 1965; paperback, New York: Schocken, 1966), pp. 108, 111.

28. Arnold J. Band, "Kafka and the Beiliss Affair," *Comparative Literature*, 32 (Spring 1980), 181.

29. Joyce Carol Oates, review of *The Best of Sholom Aleichem*, in *New York Times Book Review*, 8 July 1979, p. 27; Charles Neider, *The Frozen Sea: A Study of Franz Kafka* (New York: Russell and Russell, 1962), p. 194.

30. See Neider's *The Frozen Sea* for a careful study of this issue, and Walter H. Sokel, "Freud and the Magic of Kafka's Writing," *The World of Franz Kafka*, pp. 145-188.

31. *Totem and Taboo*, in vol. 13 of *Standard Edition of the Complete Psychological Works of Sigmund Freud*, ed. J. Strachey and Anna Freud (New York: Norton, 1952), p. xv.

32. Peter Gay, *Freud, Jews and Other Germans: Masters and Victims in Modernist Culture* (Oxford and New York: Oxford University Press, 1978), p. 165.

33. Ibid., p. 109.

34. See Cynthia Ozick, *The Pagan Rabbi and Other Stories* (New York: Knopf, 1971). I am indebted to her interview on the BBC's series, "Three American Writers," Radio Three, 18 May 1980, for background information.

35. Ozick, "America: Towards Yavneh," *Judaism*, 19 (1970), 273, 276, 278.

36. "The informal liturgical culture rapidly burgeoning among American Jews is as much the result of the restoration of Israel as it is of the Holocaust. And yet it appears to have its own life, it is not merely an aftermath or backwash, it has an urge not to repeat or recapitulate, but to go forward, —as, at an earlier Yavneh, Yochanan ben Zakkai plunged into the elaboration of Aggadah and preserved Torah by augmenting it. It seems to me that we are ready to re-think ourselves in America now, to preserve ourselves by a new culture-making." Ibid., pp. 279-280. But see the discussion by Edward Alexander, *The Resonance of Dust: Essays on Holocaust Literature and Jewish Fate* (Columbus: Ohio State Univesity Press, 1979), pp. 139-141, for a sympathetic yet skeptical treatment, and Ruth Wisse's comments in "American Jewish Writing, Act II," *Commentary*, 61:6 (June 1976), p. 43.

37. Adele Wiseman, *Crackpot* (Toronto: McClelland and Stewart, 1974).

38. Wisse, "American Jewish Writing," pp. 43-44. Also see Robert Alter, *After the Tradition* (New York: Dutton, 1969).

39. See Ozick's story "The Butterfly and the Traffic Light," in *The Pagan Rabbi*, pp. 207-218.

40. "Envy," *The Pagan Rabbi*, pp. 39-100.

41. T. Carmi and Dan Pagis, *Selected Poems*, trans. Stephen Mitchell (London: Penguin, 1976).

42. Amos Oz, "Crusade," *Commentary*, 52:2 (August 1971), 42-72. This story has been issued along with another in *Unto Death* (New York: Harcourt, Brace, 1975).

8. City Premises

1. Norman Hampson, *A Social History of the French Revolution* (Toronto: University of Toronto Press), 1966, p. 205.

2. Joyce Carol Oates in *New York Times Book Review*, 8 July 1979, p. 27.

3. Alfred Kazin, *A Walker in the City* (New York: Harcourt, Brace and World, 1951), p. 58.

4. Daniel Aaron, "From Communism to *Commentary*," in *The

Ghetto and Beyond: Essays on Jewish Life in America, ed. Peter I. Rose (New York: Random House, 1969), p. 266.

5. Johanna Kaplan, *O My America* (New York: Harper and Row, 1980), p. 225.

6. Isaac Rosenfeld, *Passage from Home* (New York: Meridian, 1961), p. 118.

7. Ibid., pp. 279-280.

8. See Sinclair's recent collection, *Hearts of Gold* (London: Allison and Busby, 1979).

9. Gunther Barth, *City People: The Rise of Modern City Culture in Nineteenth Century America* (Oxford: Oxford University Press, 1980), esp. chap. 5.

10. Kazin, *New York Jew* (New York: Knopf, 1978), p. 295.

11. Milton Gordon, "Marginality and the Jewish Intellectual," *The Ghetto and Beyond*, p. 489. Also see Milton M. Goldberg, "A Qualification of the Marginal Man Theory," *American Sociological Review*, 6 (1941), 52-58.

12. See under "Yiddish," in *Encyclopedia Judaica* (Jerusalem: Keter, 1974), XVI, 792b. Also see Max Weinreich, "Yiddishkayt and Yiddish: On the Impact of Religion on Language in Ashkenazic Jewry," in *Readings in the Sociology of Language*, ed. Joshua A. Fishman (The Hague: Mouton, 1968), pp. 382-413.

13. Hutchins Hapgood, *The Spirit of the Ghetto*, new ed. with preface and notes by Harry Golden (New York: Schocken, 1966).

14. Michel Serres, *L'Intérfèrence* (Paris: Editions de Minuit, 1972), p. 157.

15. "Gedali," *Collected Stories of Isaac Babel*, trans. Walter Morison (New York: Meridian, 1960), p. 72.

16. Dan Miron argues as I do in Chapter 5 that this strategy is central to Sholom Aleichem's work. See his *Sholom Aleykhem: Person, Persona, Presence* (The Uriel Weinreich Memorial Lecture I, Columbia University, New York, YIVO Institute for Jewish Research, 1972), p. 24.

17. Richard Poirier, *A World Elsewhere: The Place of Style in American Literature* (New York: Oxford University Press, 1966).

18. Philip Roth, *The Ghost Writer* (New York: Farrar, Straus, and Giroux, 1979), p. 10.

19. Rachel Erteil, *Le roman Juif Americain: Une écriture minoritaire* (Paris: Payot, 1980), p. 28.

20. Sol Gittleman, *From Shtetl to Suburbia* (Boston: Beacon Press, 1978), p. 156.

21. Lynn Luria-Sukenick, "Beatrice Reveals a Dream About the

Future, About the Ones Who Will Not Escape," *Pequod*, 12 (1981), 74.

22. Jean Vallely, in *Esquire*, 10 October 1978, p. 10.

23. For a full discussion of the problem of Jewish identity, ethnicity, and modernity, see Kevin Avruch, *American Immigrants in Israel: Social Identities and Change* (Chicago: University of Chicago Press, 1981), esp. chaps. 6 and 7.

24. Kaplan, *O My America*, pp. 205-206.

Index